Murders & Misdeeds
Angus and Dundee
1765–1900

Forbes Inglis

The Pinkfoot Press
Brechin, 2013

Published 2013 in Scotland by
The Pinkfoot Press
1 Pearse Street, Brechin, Angus DD9 6JR

ISBN 978 1874012 62 7

Typeset and designed at The Pinkfoot Press
Printed by Scandinavian Book

Contents

* The year given is when the offence took place

3

Illustrations

Introduction

Looking for a new topic for talks to local groups, I took up the stories of capital punishment in nineteenth-century Angus and quickly discovered that many people, particularly the ladies I have to say, seemed to enjoy, if that is the word, listening to tales of murders and public hangings.

Of course, many of those who paid the ultimate penalty were undoubtedly guilty but others were found guilty and hanged on circumstantial evidence that today, without the benefit of forensic science, would certainly make the convictions unsafe.

Other unfortunates were simply mentally ill, more in need of treatment than judicial punishment, while others, some possibly guilty, were acquitted.

Even today, despite the use of modern forensic techniques, we still find many convictions are deemed unsafe.

This book tells the stories of some of those charged with capital offences in Angus and Dundee in the eighteenth and nineteenth centuries, along with what is known about the men whose job it was to dispatch them if they were found guilty.

Acknowledgements

My thanks to the staff at Aberdeen City and Aberdeenshire Archives, the Local Studies Department of Aberdeenshire Libraries, Angus Archives, the Local History Section at Dundee Central Library, Montrose Library, and Willie Macfarlane of Tayside Police Museum for their patience and assistance in dealing with my inquiries and making the information I needed available. Thanks too to Alex Whyte of Forfar who put me on the track of James Robertson and the simple stone memorial at the old prison there.

Without their help this book simply couldn't have been written.

Capital Punishment

Executing felons for the commission of crime has a long history. Often justice was administered locally and it was only on the introduction of the Heritable Jurisdictions (Scotland) Act 1746 that the landowners in the country districts and magistrates in the towns lost the power to execute wrongdoers.

Other than hanging, the best known form of execution was probably witch burning, which continued up until the original legislation, including the Scottish Witchcraft Act of 1563, was repealed by the Witchcraft Act 1735. In fact witches were generally strangled first so the burning was largely symbolic.

Upper class criminals were beheaded and, between 1565 and 1710, the Maiden, a piece of equipment similar to a guillotine, was used to execute other criminals.

From that time until the nineteenth century there were many crimes, although not as many as in England, for which the penalty was death. Offences, other than murder, that carried the death penalty in the latter part of the nineteenth century included rape, robbery, burglary, housebreaking, forgery, sheep, deer, cattle or horse stealing and fire raising, although even then execution was generally reserved for murder.

Eventually, public hangings became the normal way of ending the lives of those found guilty of capital offences. Unfortunately, in the early days, hanging generally resulted in death by strangulation.

At the time, the authorities saw hanging as a deterrent, just as some people still do today. Not only that, justice also had to be seen to be done, no doubt as a lesson to others. Nevertheless, the practice of public execution was finally brought to an end in 1868 and in 1965 hanging was suspended for five years before being fully abolished for most crimes in 1969. (Treason, arson in Royal dockyards, spying and a number of other crimes were still punishable by death up until the final years of the twentieth century.)

Public Executions

Although the idea of public executions might seem uncivilised to us today for several hundred years they were considered almost as a form of entertainment so, for the lower classes who had few pleasures in their lives, a hanging represented a day out.

This in turn meant large crowds which would have attracted people with wares to sell, sideshows, conjurors, conmen, pickpockets and other unsavoury characters. As a result they were festive occasions, other than for the unfortunate who was to be hanged, more like a fair than an object lesson, although contemporary reports almost invariably describe the crowd as being hushed and respectful and suggest that those attending were from the lower orders or even strangers.

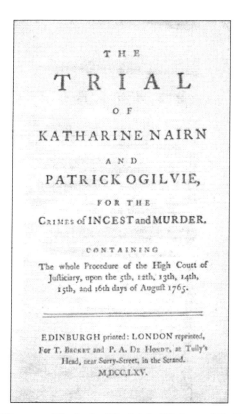

T H E

T R I A L

O F

KATHARINE NAIRN

A N D

PATRICK OGILVIE,

FOR THE

CRIMES of INCEST and MURDER.

CONTAINING

The whole Procedure of the High Court of
Jufticiary, upon the 5th, 12th, 13th, 14th,
15th, and 16th days of Auguft 1765.

EDINBURGH printed: LONDON reprinted,
For T. Becket and P. A. De Hondt, at Tully's
Head, near Sorry-Street, in the Strand.
M,DCC,LXV.

1 *Title page of the book of the trial of Nairn and Ogilvie*

The case of Patrick Ogilvie and his sister-in-law, Katharine Nairn, accused of incest and murder at Eastmiln, a small estate in the parish of Glenylla (Glen Isla, the most westerly of the five Angus glens), would be a tabloid sensation even today.

The players in this drama were Thomas Ogilvie and his wife Katharine, Thomas's brother Patrick and Mrs Ogilvie senior who was known, as was common practice at the time, by the courtesy title of Lady Eastmiln, Anne Clark, a cousin of the family, and three female servants. The youngest son of the family, Alexander, was studying medicine in Edinburgh.

Now the house at Eastmiln was relatively small and the walls and ceilings were extremely thin giving little or no privacy to any of the occupants, a factor that added to the intrigue.

Katharine Nairn had been just nineteen years old when she married Thomas Ogilvie, a man more than twenty years older than her, on 30 January 1765.

If Patrick Ogilvie was to be the apparent catalyst in this intrigue then Anne Clark was to play a major role too. She had arrived at Eastmiln, not just to see Thomas and his new bride and Patrick, who had only recently returned to Scotland, but also to try to effect a reconciliation with the family for Alexander who had been shunned for marrying beneath him. Later, giving her evidence for the prosecution at the trial, Miss Clark was to prove the star witness.

Despite the age gap and the fact that Thomas, a forty-year-old 'bonnet laird' (a small landowner), seems to have been somewhat set in his ways while his bride came from a more aristocratic, although relatively poor, family, the couple seemed to have had a genuine affection for each other.

Little might have changed had fate not brought Patrick, a lieutenant in the 89th Regiment of Foot, back home to Eastmiln to recuperate after becoming ill while serving in the East Indies.

Patrick seems to have been everything that his brother wasn't – younger, fitter and healthier – and, in the circumstances, it is easy to understand how the young Katharine might have become attracted to the dashing young lieutenant who shared her joy of living and youthful outlook on life.

The big questions were whether they actually became lovers and did one or both decide to murder Thomas?

The Crown case was based on the belief that Katharine had grown tired of her husband and had, contrary to the strict laws of incest of the time, formed a relationship with her brother-in-law, Patrick, before deciding to murder her husband by giving him poison.

Patrick, for his part, was said to have obtained laudanum and arsenic for her, drugs which were readily available and were frequently used as tonics and in the treatment of skin problems and other ailments.

Within days of Thomas's death on 6 June 1765, his youngest brother, Alexander, returned to the house and immediately cancelled the funeral, claiming that his brother had been murdered. He informed the authorities and the plot, if it actually existed, was soon revealed.

The two suspects were arrested on 14 June and sent to Edinburgh a week later before being indicted for murder and incest on 20 July:

> ... THAT WHEREAS by the law of God, and the laws of this and all other well governed realms, the crime of INCEST, committed betwixt a man and the wife of his brother, especially when such crime is committed within the dwelling-house of the injured husband, where the offenders were cherished and entertained by him with confidence and trust, is a heinous crime, and most severely punishable ... AND ALSO, by the same holy law of God, ... all wilful HOMICIDE or MURDER, especially when perpetrated by poison, and above all, when such murder is committed under trust, or upon a person to whom fidelity and affection are due by the most sacred ties, is also a crime of the most heinous nature.

Given the moral outlook of the period it is likely that the allegation of incest was seen as the more dreadful of the alleged crimes.

The evidence of Anne Clark was crucial to the prosecution case. If she was to be believed, the young bride must have readily accepted her as a reliable confidante almost immediately for, within weeks of her arrival, Katharine had shared her innermost thoughts on the most intimate of matters with her. Within days, she had told the witness that she wished her husband dead and that, 'if she had a dose she would give it to him' and she apparently made similar remarks on a number of other occasions.

Katharine's frank discussions with Anne Clark continued. She asked if the witness knew where she might buy poison and, although Clark suggested that such a course of action was unwise, she then offered to obtain the poison in Edinburgh.

Added to the mix was the presence in the house of the dashing Lt Ogilvie and, before long, the servants had started to gossip about a possible relationship between Katharine and her brother-in-law.

According to Miss Clark she had soon became aware of over-familiarity between the two accused and noticed that Katharine was frequently alone with Patrick, a situation which led her to warn Katharine that she should be careful about her conduct.

On Sunday 19 May everyone had gone to church with the exception of the two accused, Lady Eastmiln and the witness. Clark testified that, after some conversation, the couple went upstairs together and that she heard their footsteps going into the same room and then stopping at the bed. Clark followed them upstairs and listened and was quickly convinced that Patrick and Katharine were in the same bed, 'abusing their bodies together'.

According to her account, this scandalous behaviour was repeated on the following Monday, Tuesday and Wednesday while Thomas Ogilvie was out visiting his tenants. The witness also swore that she had seen the two accused kissing and seen Patrick put his hand 'down her breast'.

Shortly afterwards, there was a falling out between the two brothers. This may have been about money but, as Anne Clark had apparently shared her 'knowledge' of Katharine's activities with Lady Eastmiln who had subsequently relayed Anne's thoughts to her son, then it might also have involved Katharine's alleged indiscretions.

Irrespective of the cause of the fallout, the inevitable result was that Thomas ordered Patrick to leave Eastmiln immediately, at which point Clark said Katharine went into his room where she threw herself onto the bed and cried.

To drive the point home, the witness then declared that on the day Patrick left Katharine had asked him to get poison for her. Katharine was said to have continued to correspond with Patrick, imploring him to return to Eastmiln. Even Thomas, perhaps deciding he had been over hasty, wrote to invite his brother to come back but Patrick, whatever his reasons, elected to stay away.

On the day before Thomas's death the witness said that Katharine told her she had had a letter from Patrick saying that he had got poison from Alyth and would have his brother-in-law, Andrew Stewart, bring it to her. Anne Clark said she warned the accused and gave her a moral lecture.

Katharine's view, again according to the witness, was that her husband had ill-used Patrick, and that her world would be perfect if the three of them, Patrick, Katharine and Anne, were the only occupants of Eastmiln.

That evening, Andrew Stewart arrived and went upstairs with Katharine. There, he passed a package to her and she locked it away in a drawer in a spare room.

Later, Clark said she pressed Stewart about his business there and he eventually admitted that he had brought two phials of black drugs for Katharine. She didn't get the opportunity to ask him what he meant by 'black drugs'.

When Katharine and Stewart left the house the witness took the opportunity to tell her aunt, Lady Eastmiln, everything. Clark apparently suggested telling Thomas the truth but Lady Eastmiln was of the opinion that Katharine would talk her way out of it and that they should simply warn him against taking anything from his wife in private.

Later, Clark met up with Thomas and the others and she took the opportunity to warn him that his life was in danger but said she gave no specific details. According to her account, Thomas replied that he couldn't leave as he was too busy but he understood what she meant and wouldn't take anything from his wife. Lady Eastmiln apparently had a similar conversation with the deceased.

Shortly afterwards, Anne Clark, Lady Eastmiln and Andrew Stewart talked together about how they could frustrate Katharine's evil intentions. Apparently, it was suggested that they should either get Katharine's keys from her by some means or other, or simply break into the drawer where she had put the drugs. For some reason, this course of action wasn't acceptable to the 'ever caring' Anne Clark.

The day before the murder, Thomas had an argument with his wife and consequently, he left without eating breakfast and returned in the evening complaining that he felt unwell. He went to bed without eating, although he had no sickness or convulsions then as far as Anne Clark was aware.

Unusually, Katharine made the tea the following morning and was seen in an alcove, apparently stirring the brew, before she took some up to her husband in a bowl. According to Clark's account, Thomas fell ill, purging and vomiting, almost immediately. She said he was extremely thirsty and she gave him cold water mixed with milk but he wanted only water, although he did drink some small ale.

Katharine gave Thomas a glass of wine whereupon he was violently sick again. At that point, he was complaining of 'burning at his heart', pains in his legs, difficulty in breathing and Clark said he couldn't lie still. He was said to have told one of his tenants, James Millam, that he was being poisoned.

Anne Clark, concerned as ever, wasn't aware of anyone deciding to send for a doctor so she took it upon herself to tell Andrew Stewart to fetch Mr Meik, a surgeon from Alyth. According to Anne Clark, Katharine was not keen on having a doctor attend as it would undoubtedly result in her getting 'a bad name'. Stewart was said to have told her that Meik was very discreet.

Following Thomas's death Patrick was sent for. Clark told him she knew everything and described him as showing both great concern and confusion. When the poison was mentioned, Patrick allegedly said he hadn't realised she had as barbarous a heart as to give it!

Dr Meik arrived after Thomas had died. He spoke to Katharine who was, unsurprisingly, 'in great greif and concern', although what is rather more difficult to understand is her request that 'whatever he might think to be the cause of her husband's death, he should conceal it from the world'.

Nevertheless, Dr Meik left the house, apparently without giving any indication as to what he believed had caused the death.

For some reason, Clark had spoken to a surgeon who said he took laudanum for gout, and he had told her it was safe if used 'cautiously'. Quite why she should have such a conversation is unclear.

Under cross-examination she told the court she knew nothing of Thomas being enthusiastic about being rid of her, saying it was another member of the family, Marion Ogilvie, prompted by Katharine, who had dismissed her. This was despite the fact that she and Katharine were such 'good' friends.

It would appear that Katharine and Patrick certainly enjoyed each other's company, although much of the evidence as to how intimate their friendship was appears to have been little more than hearsay.

A prosecution witness who lived nearby, David Rattray, told the court that he

> did hear it talked in the country, that Mrs Ogilvie, the pannel (accused), and Lieutenant Ogilvie the other pannel … walked out together without others in their company.

Rather more damning however, he said that on one occasion he had seen them personally, arm in arm and kissing.

Similar evidence was given by another neighbour, David Lamar, who had 'heard that Mr Ogilvie liked Mrs Ogilvie too well, loved one another too well' at the time when Lt Ogilvie had been asked to leave Eastmiln. Witness thought it would have been about two weeks before Thomas Ogilvie's death. He said he too had seen them, arm-in-arm and with their arms about each other's necks, even with Miss Clark and the Laird present. If that is true then both of the accused, even if guilty of nothing more than being over-friendly, had been reckless in the extreme.

Even more damning evidence, particularly for the period, came from John Gilloch, a carpenter who had been instructed to fit a new lock on a drawer in Patrick's bedroom. Patrick was still in bed when Katherine came in and proceeded to address him in familiar terms and put her hand on his body, although the witness couldn't say if her hand was above or below the bedclothes.

Just as Katharine was leaving Patrick kicked off the covers and the witness 'could judge whether he was a man or a woman'. He did admit under cross-examination that Katharine wouldn't have seen this as she was leaving the room by then and had her back to Patrick.

Other witnesses, particularly those who had been servants at Eastmiln, had similar stories to tell.

The following witness, despite protests from the defence about her character, was Katharine Campbell, a serving-lass dismissed by Katharine Ogilvie for stealing. She was aged twenty-seven and unmarried. A native Gaelic speaker she had a poor command of English and was required to give her evidence through an interpreter.

The witness said she had seen Patrick kissing Katharine on a number of occasions and thought 'he showed too great fondness for his sister in law'. She told him that and he replied that 'his brother desired him to be fond of her, to keep her cheerful in the beginning'.

But Katharine Campbell had an even more damning tale to tell. While Thomas had been away for a few days she had made up two separate rooms for Patrick and Katharine. Katharine's room was immediately above the kitchen where the witness herself slept. On one occasion she heard Mrs Ogilvie cry out, 'Oh fy, fy', and 'heard the bed moving as if somebody had been stirring in it'.

When she went to make the beds the following day there was no indication that Patrick's bed had been slept in. If that is true then Patrick showed a distinct lack of foresight.

The witness said she had offered to sleep in her mistress's room (the practice of servants sleeping on the floor of individual family members seems to have been common in the household), but was told that wasn't necessary.

She had found an unmade bed only once, as on other occasions Patrick's bed had apparently been slept in.

A similar tale was told by Elizabeth Sturrock, a maidservant aged twenty-three. She swore that she had heard the footsteps of the two accused in the same room and also claimed to have heard breathing, as if the two were in the same bed.

Sturrock also gave evidence that Katharine Nairn was upset when Patrick was ordered out of the house and said she took a number of letters from her to Patrick

Later in her evidence, she insisted that her master had been in good health and that, in fact, she had never known him to be in bad health. She said she had been sick and confined to her bed in the kitchen on the morning of her master's death. Katharine Nairn had come into the kitchen and told her that she had given the master his breakfast and told her that she was to say she had got her's too, even although that wasn't true. Later, her mistress had sent Ann Samson, another servant, in with her tea.

When her master was in the kitchen he had said he was ill and her mistress had said he should go to bed.

Later, she told the court, she was at her master's bedside. He was very ill and drinking a lot. She was there between 10:00 and 11:00 am when Lady Eastmiln and Andrew Stewart came into the room and it was then that her master said he had been poisoned and 'that woman had done it'. By that she thought he meant Katharine Nairn. She said Lady Eastmiln reproved him for saying so but he had insisted that it was true.

Her mistress then came to spend some time with her husband but refused to stay with him for long, saying she did not like to see dying people. After his death witness thought she showed little grief.

When her mistress heard that the Sheriff of Forfar had been sent for she asked the witness to say she had seen her mix the tea and that she, the witness, had tasted it before it was given to the deceased. Patrick

14

Ogilvie was there at that point and he told the witness to do as her mistress had said.

On the day after Thomas had died, Ann Samson had told Mrs Stewart, the deceased's sister, that she had seen the bowl given to Thomas in a cupboard in the kitchen and she had noticed something greasy on the bottom of it. Mrs Stewart had put some broth in it which was fed to the dog who seemed none the worse for the experience.

One of the things that makes much of the prosecution evidence so difficult to assess is the fact that many of the prosecution witnesses, particularly those employed or previously employed at Eastmiln, had discussed the trial amongst themselves and, perhaps even more damningly, with Anne Clark.

Almost invariably, those resident or employed at Eastmiln swore that they had never known Thomas Ogilvie to be ill or suffer from any form of sickness before. Strangely enough, several defence witnesses swore that Thomas had had several bouts of illness in the past, including one episode just days before his death.

In fact, George Spalding, who was married to a member of the Ogilvie family, gave evidence that he had written to Katharine's mother, Lady Nairn, in February saying that Eastmiln should be made over legally to Katharine because of Thomas's poor health. Over the years, Thomas had complained of 'heart-cholic, a pain in his stomach and a short cough which seldom left him'.

Another area of doubt is that Lady Eastmiln had been present when Anne Clark 'heard' the two accused upstairs in the same bed. Although she was one of a considerable number of defence witnesses not permitted to give evidence, apparently she had heard nothing untoward.

In considering Anne Clark's evidence we need to be aware that she had a vested interest in breaking up the marriage of Thomas and Katharine, although the drama that had subsequently developed must have been beyond her wildest dreams.

She had cohabited for a time with Alexander Ogilvie and she was said to have taken 'every occasion to publicise the most scandalous falsehoods, calculated to create a misunderstanding between Katherine and her husband' as part of a plot to destabilise the Ogilvie family and have her former paramour allowed back into the fold.

So, despite her evidence giving the impression that she had only the good of the family at heart, the opposite is probably true.

James Millam gave evidence that Thomas had complained to him that he couldn't get any peace in his house for Anne Clark and that 'he wished her away'. In fact, such was the Laird's strength of feeling about her that he gave the witness ten shillings (50p) to give to her 'for her journey'. A few days later, he saw Katharine Nairn giving her money too.

Of course, Alexander himself had an exceptionally strong motive for driving a wedge between Thomas and Katharine, and if Patrick was hanged that would be a bonus. He would then be rid of his two brothers and, if Katharine failed to produce an heir, that would be even better as he would then inherit everything.

Following the death, Patrick, as heir under the inheritance law of the time, made the necessary funeral arrangements and Anne Clark left Eastmiln. Despite her protestations that she had no contact with anyone, her former lover, Alexander Ogilvie, appeared at Eastmiln on the morning of the funeral when he announced that there would be no interment as he was convinced that his brother hadn't died from natural causes.

Alexander then insisted on sending for Dr Ogilvie from Forfar and Drs Ramsay and Meik from Alyth. Katharine Nairn was said to be most upset, crying and wringing her hands at this time, although given the sudden arrival of Alexander and his accusation of murder that would be hardly surprising.

Largely on the strength of Alexander's unsupported allegations, Katharine and Patrick were taken into custody on 14 June and made declarations before the Sheriff at Forfar before being transferred to Edinburgh.

Within days, Alexander had sold off the farm stock, apparently, and no doubt fraudulently, on the authority of Patrick.

All three doctors appeared at the trial and gave evidence that they had inspected the body six days after the death. Each medical man gave evidence that parts of the body had been black, scarcely surprising as putrefaction would by then have been a factor, and declared that they also had concerns about the state of the tongue.

Dr Meik, who had first seen the body within two hours of death, thought that the swollen tongue he noticed six days later might be a sign of poisoning but he subsequently admitted that he had no experience of poisoning and said it had been Alexander who had suggested the possibility of poison to him. He did however say that on both occasions,

Katharine had asked him to keep the cause of death secret.

Meik had also talked with Dr Ramsay about the possibility of them opening up the body for further examination but this suggestion was vetoed by Alexander who wanted Dr Ogilvie to be present as well.

Ramsay's evidence was similar to that of Dr Meik. He felt the discolouration might indicate the presence of poison but he admitted he had no experience of such deaths other than the knowledge that arsenic poisoning led to vomiting and evacuating downwards. These symptoms could, particularly in those days, have been easily confused with death caused by a ruptured gastric ulcer.

Dr Ogilvie arrived after his two colleagues had left. He drew no conclusions from the appearance of the body other than that most features were due to decomposition, a factor he thought made the body too putrid to open safely. He agreed that Patrick didn't ask him to carry out a post-mortem but said that, on the other hand, he hadn't ordered him not too.

So, there might have been a post-mortem had it not been for Alexander's refusal to permit that to happen without Dr Ogilvie being present.

Patrick had admitted getting some salts and laudanum for Katharine and said these were in his sea-chest which had been kept in Dundee. Unfortunately for Patrick, James Carnegie, a surgeon in Brechin, had told the court that he had sold arsenic to the accused, who wanted it 'to kill dogs that were spoiling the game'.

Even the evidence that the substance was arsenic was in itself doubtful as Dr Carnegie could only recall that he had bought it a long time before and that it was a substance that could be used to kill rats!

Robert Smith, a surgeon called by the defence, gave evidence that a deceased might exhibit the stated symptoms without having had arsenic. In 1765 there was no proper scientific test for arsenic and without a post-mortem it was impossible to ascertain the cause of Thomas's death.

The symptoms of arsenic poisoning tend to follow a regular pattern. The reaction to a large dose of the poison is vomiting and diarrhoea followed by severe dehydration and the skin becomes cold and clammy. Another symptom is the presence of muscle spasm, particularly in the calves. Eventually, the patient falls into a coma and dies of heart failure. While Thomas seems to have exhibited some if not all of those symptoms they are also symptoms of other ailments.

The difficulty for the medical men of the eighteenth and early-nineteenth centuries was that many of the symptoms were also signs of various ailments including food poisoning and at a time when standards of hygiene were lax to say the least, that was often the most likely cause of death.

Not having access to today's scientific tests and knowledge the doctors of the time could never be sure as to the cause of death in such instances, a fact that made arsenic a popular choice for those with murder in mind. Little wonder then that arsenic was often called 'inheritance powder'.

Curiously enough, the doctors' interpretations of the 'signs' of poisoning exhibited by Thomas's body may have had some truth in them, although their thinking was probably based on folklore rather than scientific fact.

The presence of arsenic causes the tongue to go black, while taking substantial doses regularly over a long period can cause thickening of the skin, and occasionally bruising, particularly on the palms of the hands and the soles of the feet. After death, these areas can become dark or discoloured so that their 'diagnoses' might have had some substance.

On the other hand, Thomas's health, despite the 'evidence' to the contrary, was undoubtedly poor and it is equally possible that he died of natural or at least innocent causes. Certainly, Thomas had experienced sickness, diarrhoea, severe thirst and muscle pain but there was no concrete evidence that he had been poisoned. (Many years later, the grave of Thomas Ogilvie was opened in error and his body was found to be extremely well preserved, a tribute to the preservative action of arsenic perhaps.)

Given the vested interests of witnesses and the lack of real evidence of poison, there should have been considerable doubt but both parties were found guilty of incest by a majority, while Katharine was found guilty, again by a majority, of murder. Patrick was found guilty of being art and part (the Scots legal term for aiding and abetting) to the crime. In truth, the whole conduct of the trial had been shambolic with jury members taking breaks or speaking to witnesses and the prosecutors when they felt like it during the proceedings. It was also a fact that, despite the case being heard before a number of judges, at one point only one was on the bench.

The members of the jury had also become impatient and as a result the defence case had to be cut short with the evidence of only ten of one hundred and eight potential defence witnesses heard.

Despite an appeal based on the biased nature of the hearing both of the accused were sentenced to hang.

Katharine's advocate then advised the court that his client was pregnant and after this was confirmed by five midwives, her execution was postponed. Interestingly enough, our current scientific knowledge would allow us to establish who the father of the child was, a fact that might have made her appear more, or less, guilty, depending on the outcome.

She gave birth to a daughter on 27 January 1766 but when the Court met again on 10 March to pronounce the sentence of death it was accepted that she was still not strong enough to be brought before them. (The child died just weeks later.)

The sentence against Patrick Ogilvie was respited four times and it was 13 November before he was finally brought to the gallows.

On the days before his execution, Patrick continued to profess his innocence and remarked that 'his brother, who had undertaken the prosecution, had behaved in a manner undeservedly rigorous', yet he (Patrick) died in charity with all mankind.

On the scaffold Patrick was about to face the drop when the noose slipped and he fell to the ground. He was immediately grabbed and hauled back up the ladder by officials and the rope placed around his neck for the second time. This time the hangman, Isaac Gibbs, made no mistake and Patrick was left hanging until he died.

In the meantime, Katharine was confined in the Tolbooth awaiting her fate but she had friends and relatives in high places who were willing to help her.

Her uncle, Sir William Nairn, a future Lord of Justiciary, had arranged for her to escape, disguised as one of the midwives, on the night of Saturday 15 March 1766. Sir William's clerk, James Bremner, a future Solicitor of Stamps, was waiting at the foot of Horse Wynd to bundle her into a carriage.

There are a numerous versions as to Katharine's fate from that moment. According to one source, Bremner escorted her to Dover where she took ship for France. From there she was said to have travelled to Holland where she married again and had a large family before later entering a convent. According to this version she died in England in the 1800s.

Another possibility is that she entered a convent almost immediately following her escape, while yet another source suggests she left France for America where she married and died at an advanced age, surrounded by her large family.

Two rewards, each of £100, were put up for information leading to her recapture, but neither was ever claimed.

An alternative account of Katharine's escape, copied in longhand from the *Newgate Calendar* in 1834, suggests that she escaped dressed in the uniform of an officer and was met by an old footman who had been a long term employee of the family. The pair were then said to have travelled south in a post-chaise. Despite Katharine escaping at around 9:00 pm it was, apparently noon the following day before her absence was noted by which time the pair were faraway.

Katharine then apparently paid the master of a Dutch fishing smack £50 to take her to Holland but bad weather forced him to turn back and she was landed back on English soil. Undaunted, Katharine travelled to Dover where she caught the Packet Boat to Calais and 'no authentic accounts respecting her have transpired since that period' – an ending that seems more likely than any of the other stories.

While it is possible that the relationship between Katharine and Patrick was purely platonic and that Thomas wasn't murdered at all there may be another side to Katharine's character as there have also been suggestions that she wasn't perhaps as innocent as she seemed.

Although I could find no evidence of such behaviour at least one source suggests she had several lovers before she married Thomas and that two of them fought a duel over her. Presumably Katharine favoured one over the other because she is said to have sneaked up behind her 'second choice' and stabbed him. To his credit, the victor refused to finish the unfortunate man off whereupon Katharine apparently tried to strangle the wounded man with her bare hands.

Another of Katharine's lovers was said to have been found at the foot of a steep gully with his neck broken. The question would appear to be the perennial – did he fall or was he pushed?

The same source also suggests that having escaped justice she took several lovers during her time on the continent and that when she grew tired of them, she poisoned them too!

Alexander failed to benefit from the fruits of Eastmiln. Having married once he obviously liked the idea and he married the daughter of an Army officer, unfortunately without divorcing or waiting for his first wife to die.

As a result, he was charged with bigamy and banished for seven years.

He was however, allowed a two-month respite to put his affairs in order during which time he fell from the upper floor of a house in Edinburgh and was killed.

There might have been those in Glen Isla who were in no way surprised at any of this.

The local minister, Rev James Mitchell, was expelled from his charge on 17 April 1740 for his 'scandalous and immoral life'.

It had been alleged that he had seduced one of his parishioners and, despite his denials, he was removed from his post. Now the Ogilvie sons had been leading figures in the campaign to remove him and, in a less than Christian moment during his final sermon, he cursed them from the pulpit:

If these men die the death common to men, God hath not spoken by me.

Thomas had only inherited Eastmiln after the death of his father and two older brothers.

His father, an enthusiastic supporter of the Jacobite cause, was imprisoned in Edinburgh castle and he fell, fracturing his skull, while attempting to escape.

The eldest son hanged himself in a sheep-cot. His first attempt failed, ironically given Patrick's fate, because the drop wasn't long enough, but he was obviously a man of dogged determination for he dug out a hole with his feet in order to see the deed through.

William, the next in line, was crushed between two ships and we already know the fate of Thomas, Patrick and Alexander.

Mr Mitchell's curse was complete.

Andrew Low was the last man in Scotland to be sentenced to death by a sheriff. Little more than a petty offender, Low, who was already a well known thief by the time he was nine, was just twenty years old when Sheriff-Depute Patrick Chalmers condemned him to death for housebreaking on 28 January 1785.

Low's father died before he was born and he was raised by his widowed mother who was unable to control her son.

Even as a youngster Low seems to have been 'a wild hallicate loon' (a wild and irresponsible youth) and whether a father's firm hand, in those days no doubt applied to his person, might have changed his life for the better it is impossible to say.

An eccentric old woman, Lizzie Kinmond, lived near Low and his mother. Indeed, had Lizzie lived a hundred years earlier she might have been executed herself for she was credited with having supernatural powers. Young girls came from all over the surrounding area to get her to tell their fortunes but that was one of her more benign gifts for Lizzie was said to have 'the evil eye' and if she put a curse on anyone they were doomed in one way or another.

Now Lizzie's pride and joy, more of a pet than anything else, was her speckled hen. The hen was 'clockin' or, in other words, broody. A clockin hen doesn't lay while in that state but wants chickens and Lizzie had put thirteen fertile eggs in a nest for it to hatch.

Low, seeing an opportunity to make some easy money, stole the hen and sold it to a local ale-wife.

Lizzie was furious as he hadn't just stolen her hen but effectively murdered the thirteen chicks that had been about to hatch. She prophesied:

> He'll no dee [die] in his bed, an that there'll be as mony lookin on at his death as ther wir feathers on my speckled chuckie's body.

Nothing could be proved so the affair of the 'clockin' hen went no further.

Just weeks after the theft Low stole a half-crown coin from the kirk collection but it was found by his mother who beat him until he confessed where it had come from. She returned it to the minister who, impressed by her honesty, agreed to take no further action on the matter.

Perhaps that might have changed Low's ways but his mother died when he was only twelve. That removed the final restraint on his behaviour and he soon slipped deeper and deeper into a criminal life, although he was caught and publicly whipped on a number of occasions.

Just months before his execution Low met a respectable young woman, Jessie Smart, who proved the old adage that love is indeed blind. She either believed that she could reform him or simply didn't see him as a criminal because he invariably assured her of his innocence.

Towards the end of 1784 Low broke into the house of Andrew Lindsay, merchant, at Slateford and then the house of John Bailie, shoemaker, of Mainsbank, Kinnell.

Following the robberies he spent a few days in an alehouse in Arbroath before returning to Forfar where he met up with some of his unsavoury friends at Robert Young's alehouse in the Osnaburg Pend. Fuelled with alcohol and with money to burn Low offered to treat his friends to a night out at the local theatre.

There, the overly-refreshed Low proceeded to draw attention to himself by calling out and heckling the cast until several members of the audience were sufficiently outraged to demand his removal.

Unfortunately for Low, one of those present was the local procurator-fiscal, Mr Wyllie, who, earlier that day, had been informed that Low was suspected of carrying out the break-ins. Wyllie discreetly contacted the Town's Officers who came and arrested Low.

As Low was being taken to the tolbooth his friends attacked the officers and he was able to make his escape. He ran until he reached Montreathmont Forest, halfway to Montrose, where he spent days without food before he was finally caught and taken back to Forfar.

Both Lindsay and Bailie came to Forfar, along with a number of others who had bought some of the stolen items, to make statements.

On 21 January 1785 Low was brought to trial before Sheriff Chalmers and a jury of fifteen gentlemen of the county who, after hearing the evidence, unanimously brought in a verdict of guilty. For some reason, possibly the need to bring an executioner from Aberdeen to Forfar to act as doomster, it was the following week before sentence was read out.

The sentence itself was straightforward enough. Low was sentenced to 'be hung by the neck until dead, on the west end of the Hill of Forfar, on Saturday 19th March'. In addition it was ordained that 'the said

Andrew Low's haill moveable goods and gear be escheat and inbrought to His Majesty's use'. (i.e. All of Low's moveable estate was to be forfeit and become the property of the Crown.)

In those days, Saturday was market day in Forfar but a public hanging would undoubtedly have added to the numbers thronging the main street.

As was the custom, Low had been visited every day by the local minister, Mr Bruce, and although he had generally been 'patient and penitent' he continued to protest his innocence.

On the last stroke of twelve noon, Lang Strang, the Steeple bell, began to toll the death knell and an eerie silence descended on the several thousand onlookers who had crammed into the area around the Cross. There was invariably a certain ceremonial aspect as regards public executions. On this occasion, a cart, already carrying a rough casket for the body, stopped at the outside stair leading up to the Tolbooth and Low, the hangman – John Chapman or Robert Welsh depending on the source – and Mr Bruce all clambered aboard and took a seat on the coffin.

The cart set off as part of a procession with the Town's Officers, carrying their halberds (long-shafted axes), Provost Ure, Bailies Watt & Dickson, and Lieutenant John Watt, the burgh treasurer, leading the way, with one hundred and fifty special constables, brandishing their truncheons to keep the crowd from getting too close, bringing up the rear.

With the crowd following on behind, the procession made its way out of the town, stopping only at the Toll House, so that the condemned man could, in keeping with ancient custom, have his last drink. After Low had taken his final drink the procession moved through the fields known as Gallowshade to the gallows erected on the Hill of Balmashanner. There a laverock (skylark) hovered above the condemned man's head, singing sweetly, and continued to do so until the wretched Low met his end.

Mr Bruce led the assembly in prayer before Provost Ure asked Low if he had anything to say.

Low nodded.

> I want to tell you, lads an fat I hae to say is juist this, that I'm hangit innocent; no that I've been a guid bairn a my days, but th' only thing that has troubled me, an aften I cudna get sleep for thinkin o't, wis th' stealin of Lizzie Kinmond's clockin hen.

There, followed the singing of psalm 118, still known in the district many years later as 'Andrew Low's psalm', which Low is said to have sung with considerable gusto until, at verse 20, he pointed his finger at the gibbet. Verse 20 reads:

> This is the gate of God, by it
> The just shall enter in;
> Thee will I praise for thou me heard'st
> And hast my safety been.

The hangman then adjusted the rope before the cart, on which the condemned man had been standing, was driven off and Andrew Low swung into eternity.

Above his head, the laverock suddenly stopped singing and flew away while down below, his sweetheart, Jessie Smart, and another young woman, Jean Starker, reputedly an old flame of Low's, both fainted.

So Lizzie Kinmond's prophecy that the number of people who would view Low's death would be greater than the number of feathers on her hen's body came true but there were many there who believed that the laverock's disappearance at the very moment of his execution signified his innocence.

Guilty of that particular offence or not, Low was little more than a petty criminal, and a fairly poor one at that.

2 *Andrew Low was hanged at Balmashanner, now the site of Forfar's War Memorial*

1801   John Watt

John Watt, a weaver, was tried and convicted of theft by housebreaking at the Circuit Court in Perth. He was hanged, the first such execution in Dundee for over a century, on 12 June 1801.

The Edinburgh Advertiser of the time reported that the Lords of Justiciary were of the view that all criminals should be executed in the place where they had committed their crime adding, 'This is certainly a wise and salutary measure'.

Obviously, the idea was that this would be lesson to others but it did nothing to resolve the question of the towns which hosted the trials still having to bear the cost of crimes committed in other parts of the country.

1821   Margaret Tindal or Shuttleworth

At around 3:00 am on Saturday 28 April 1821, neighbours near the Inn in Castle Street in Montrose, leased by Mrs Margaret Tindal or Shuttleworth and her husband Henry, were awakened by her screams. All that they could get out of the hysterical woman was that she had got up during the night to get a drink of water and fallen over her husband's body at the foot of the stairs. According to her incoherent account, she believed that he had died having fallen down the stairs.

Several neighbours rushed to the inn where they found the lifeless body of Henry Shuttleworth lying in a pool of blood in the passage near the front door. It was immediately obvious that Henry's skull had been fractured, in 'a manner too shocking for description', according to a newspaper report of the time.

Shuttleworth was a well educated Englishman from a relatively prosperous background. His family had owned a hardware and button making business but Henry, not finding the business to his liking, had opted instead to join the marines.

Margaret Tindal's background couldn't have been any more different from her husband's. Her father had come to Montrose sometime around 1776 and he married Janet Steedsman, a chambermaid at the Turk's Head Inn.

3 *The Inn in Castle Street, Montrose, leased by Henry Shuttleworth*

Smuggling was rife in Montrose at that time and Tindal fell in with a smuggler called William Japp and, before long, the pair were working for a Captain Dangerfield, one of the most notorious smugglers on the east coast of Scotland.

Tindal was not the type to keep any sort of job, even that of a smuggler, for any length of time and before long he and Dangerfield had parted company.

After a spell as gardener at Little Mill he enlisted in the 81st Regiment of Foot but unsurprisingly, discipline didn't appeal to Tindal and, in an effort to get himself out of the Army, he is said to have chopped off two of his fingers. Tindal's commanding officer was wise to him however and, realising how he had come by his injuries, refused to grant him a discharge.

Faced with doing all the lowly unpleasant jobs for the rest of his enlistment Tindal deserted and returned to Montrose. The burgh was hardly the safest place for the deserter and before long Japp had to smuggle him out of the town to Lunan Bay where Dangerfield's lugger was moored.

Dangerfield took him to Gothenburg where he opened a small public house known as the Scots Inn. Men such as Tindal tend to live on the fringes of society and it was possibly no surprise when his body was found in a ditch. He had been shot through the heart.

His widow tried to make a go of the inn but before long she had to concede defeat and she returned to Scotland with her three children in 1791. Margaret was then six years old.

If her father had largely brought his troubles on himself then Margaret simply seemed fated to be unlucky.

At the age of ten she was looking after an infant. Little more than a child herself, she had taken the baby to the races on the Links. Something happened to frighten the infant and it fell from Margaret's grasp, injuring its spine so severely that it died just days later.

She later went to work at an inn owned by a Mrs Crabb who thought highly of her, describing her as 'a good servant, very punctual in her habits, clean and tidy in her person'.

From there, Margaret went to work at another inn in Dummie Ha's Wynd (now Lower Hall Street) which was owned by a former army sergeant and so was frequented by soldiers and NCOs.

Then a corporal, Henry Shuttleworth fell for the pretty young serving lass despite the fact that she was unable to read or even sign her name, and the couple married on 20 September 1806, Margaret's 21st birthday.

The couple lived in England for almost ten years during which time Henry was promoted to the rank of sergeant. Henry retired from the army in 1815 and the couple moved back to Montrose where they were able to buy a grocer's shop in Northesk Road with the savings their thrifty and sober ways had allowed them to accumulate.

Again fate took a hand, this time in the form of local brewer Henry Farquharson. He owned an inn in Castle Street, close to his brewery, and the Shuttleworths decided to take on the tenancy.

Initially, matters continued much as before but, with the business losing money and Margaret turning more and more frequently to the bottle, the relationship turned sour and Henry threatened to leave Montrose, and her, on a number of occasions.

The Montrose Review of 4 May 1821 reported:

> It appeared evident that his death had been occasioned by violence; and concurring circumstances tended to strongly attach suspicion to his wife, which, we are sorry to say, her former conduct rather strengthened than diminished. We should be sorry to violate that humane and just maxim in

our laws, which holds every person innocent till proved guilty; but we cannot resist nor disguise the emotion excited by the more than brutal treatment this kind and indulgent husband is said to have met with at the hand of the wife of his bosom; and the unnatural hardihood and want of feeling, which, we are informed, she has evinced since the melancholy catastrophe took place.

All the signs were that Henry had been murdered, apparently struck several times on the head with a blunt instrument. Margaret was the obvious suspect and she was arrested and charged with murder the following day.

Initially, she was locked up in the old Tolbooth in what is now Peel Place, just yards away from where she would be hanged. The legal paperwork was sent to Edinburgh where it was decided that there was a case to answer and consequently Mrs Shuttleworth was transferred to the Tolbooth in Forfar to await trial. She was incarcerated there from 8 June until 18 September.

On 19 September 1821 Margaret Tindal or Shuttleworth was put on trial at the Circuit Court in Perth.

The indictment stated that she did

> wickedly and feloniously assault Henry Shuttleworth, her husband ... and did inflict several severe blows upon his head with a poker, or some other instrument to the Prosecutor unknown, whereby his skull was fractured and he was mortally wounded; in consequence of which injuries the said Henry Shuttleworth did immediately or soon thereafter die, and was thereby murdered by you ... and that she did previously evince ill will against the said Henry Shuttleworth.

The panel pled Not Guilty and the evidence against her appears to have been, at best circumstantial and, at worst, conflicting.

The first witness for the prosecution was William Bennet, town officer in Montrose, who told the court he had been employed to search the Shuttleworth's premises after the murder. He said that on the Sunday he had found a poker in Tindal's bedroom, which was on the ground floor, and he identified the exhibit.

The poker, which had hair and blood on it, had been lying opposite the panel's bed. The hair was short and light in colour and he confirmed that Henry Shuttleworth, whom he knew well, had light coloured hair. Cross-examined by the defence he admitted that he saw the poker on Sunday, reported what he had seen but didn't remove it until Monday.

John Shaw, another town officer, then gave evidence that he had been with Bennet when he searched the house on the Sunday and that a small poker had been found near the chimney of a room which the panel had said was her bedroom. His evidence was that there was blood and dark hair on the poker. Although he also knew Shuttleworth he made no mention of his hair colour.

He understood that Bennet had removed the poker and passed it to the magistrates that day, although it was not examined till Monday or Tuesday. Shaw also confirmed that the house had been searched on two or three occasions but he hadn't noticed the poker then.

Mr James Burnes, a local solicitor, said the poker was there when Mrs Shuttleworth was legally examined before him but, although it was bent, he saw no sign of hair or blood on it.

Another witness, land-surveyor James Paterson, had been employed by the procurator-fiscal to make a plan of the premises. The inn lay between Bridge Street and Castle Street on one of the closes, a number of which still connect the two streets today. Paterson advised that all of the doors, other than the one onto Castle Street which had a 'sneck or lifter' operable from inside the property, could be bolted, although he accepted that it could be opened from the outside

Giving her evidence, the couple's maid, Catherine McLeod, the only other permanent resident in the premises, said that the pair lived happily enough together when her mistress was sober, but when she was drunk, which was often, she would curse, swear and throw items such as pokers and tongs at her husband.

Catherine was shown two parts of a large poker, used in the master's kitchen, which she said she had seen the panel throw at her husband. On the Friday that poker had disappeared and she couldn't shed any light on what had happened to it.

By teatime on the day of the murder the panel was intoxicated and there were a series of rows between the two. The panel had been so angry that she had put her hand through the kitchen window.

Later that night the witness had, at her master's request, put the panel to bed. She confirmed that at that point the panel was fully dressed but she had later undressed her before going out to a 'late wake'. By that stage of their relationship the Shuttleworths were sleeping apart, Henry having his bedroom upstairs.

Interestingly enough, Catherine had not told her mistress that she was going out.

When she left, sometime between 9:00 and 10:00 pm, Catherine said the deceased had had a drink but was not drunk. Before leaving, she checked if the panel was quiet and she could hear the voices of Mr Shuttleworth and his neighbour and landlord, Mr Farquharson.

The witness stayed at the wake until around 6:00 am when Mrs Farquharson and her maid appeared to tell her that her master had fallen down the stairs. She returned to the inn where the panel had said that when she got up to get herself a drink she had fallen over something which she discovered was her husband's body.

She noticed that the stairs leading to an upstairs bedroom, although not the one used by the deceased, had bloodstained footprints made by someone barefooted, on them.

By the time the witness returned the panel was dressed. Checking the premises the witness found nothing out of the ordinary. The two pieces of the large poker were later found under her master's desk but it was not unusual for such items to be put beyond the panel's use. She too had seen the small poker in the panel's bedroom but had noticed no hair or blood on it.

Asked about the relationship between the panel and the deceased she agreed that there had been talk of the deceased leaving the panel and the town altogether.

Under cross-examination the witness accepted that there had been two tumblers and a glass on the table, obviously suggesting that someone else had been present with the deceased.

She also stated that when she returned the panel didn't appear distressed and wasn't weeping. Other than saying that if she had heard him she might have saved his life she expressed no feelings. The witness did suggest that the panel was 'troubled like' and asked for the door to be closed so that she didn't have to look at the body.

The landlord, Henry Farquharson, who lived nearby, told the court that Henry Shuttleworth had given him notice that he intended to quit the inn, principally on account of his wife's conduct. It was no secret that the two no longer got along.

Farquharson also said that when he left the inn at around 10:30 pm Shuttleworth was in good health. There was no one else in the property and he hadn't heard anyone else going into the inn after he went home.

At around 4:00 am he was wakened by Mrs Shuttleworth saying,

Rise, Farquharson; Shuttleworth is lying in the entry, and I think he is dead.

The witness said he dressed and went to the scene where he saw

Shuttleworth's body lying in a pool of blood. He went to find Dr Gibson who was not at home so he had contacted Dr Hoile before returning to the inn. It was at that point he noticed bloodstains on the stairs. He asked the panel about them and she explained that she had gone upstairs looking for the servant-girl. He admitted he hadn't paid any attention to her hands.

A search of the property found nothing out of the ordinary anywhere else in the house. He also stated that the body was taken to a bedroom where it was searched, revealing nothing other than 'some silver and copper' (presumably coins).

Despite the panel's explanation for her husband's situation Farquharson didn't think that Shuttleworth's death had come about through falling downstairs, even though he would have landed on the flag stones at the bottom. Asked about Tindal herself he described her as 'partly drunk'.

On the Sunday he was at the inn again where he saw and held the small poker before it was removed on the orders of Provost Gibson but 'observed nothing particular on it'.

David Farquharson, the brother of the previous witness, gave evidence that, on the night before the murder he had locked the gate at the west end of the passage and found it to be open on the morning. He did not know who opened it.

Another witness, Mary Thorn, told of seeing Shuttleworth's body and forming the opinion that death hadn't been caused by his supposed fall. When she mentioned this to the panel she suggested that he might have moved due to the agony of his injuries. This witness also felt that the panel was 'not altogether drunk, nor was she quite sober'.

Dr Hoile had arrived at around 6:00 am and, according to his evidence, 'saw the body in the position already described'. He noticed 'much blood about the head' and, although his initial thought was that Shuttleworth had been killed by a fall, he then saw that the skull had been fractured. He believed that the skull had been subjected to three blows, possibly made by the small poker.

Hoile testified that he had seen blood on Tindal's hands and had also noticed the bloody footmarks on the stairs. (Tindal's statement said that she had lifted up her husband's head before realising he was dead, a not unreasonable explanation for the blood on her hands.)

He asked her if she had been upstairs and she initially denied it before saying she had gone looking for the servant girl. The doctor described her as agitated, although such a reaction would have hardly been surprising in the circumstances.

The doctor also confirmed that he had searched her room where he found an apron with a spot of blood on it and noticed bloody finger marks on the walls. (Other witnesses testified that when the accused came out having found the body she was wearing only a shift so if there was blood on the apron it would appear it was possibly from blood splatter.)

Another medic, Dr Crabbe, examined the body in the company of two other doctors. His opinion was that death had not been caused by a fall but by three or four blows from a blunt instrument.

Dr Gibson agreed. In his capacity as a magistrate he had gone to the inn on Saturday in the company of Robert Burnes and Henry Farquharson but he testified that he hadn't seen any blood on the small poker.

So we have evidence from some witnesses that the small poker had blood and hair on it while others gave evidence that they had seen this poker close up and had not noticed anything on it at all.

Elizabeth Croll told the court she had been in the inn on the night before Shuttleworth's death and had heard the breaking of the glass when the panel put her hand through the window. When the deceased asked the panel to look at what she had done she replied, 'If I had the big poker I would lay your harns [skull] on the floor, and let you look at that'. The witness described Tindal as staggering through drink but well aware of what she was saying.

After the closing speeches the Lord Justice Clerk summed up. He stated that

> the points for the consideration of the jury were two: 1st, Whether or not Shuttleworth's death had been accidental, or whether it had been occasioned by violence; and 2dly, If they would be of the opinion he had met his death by violence, whether the panel was the person guilty.

The following morning the jury returned with a unanimous verdict of guilty. The Lord Chief Justice ordained the panel to be hanged at Montrose, on Friday 2 November next, and her body to be given to Dr Alexander Monro, Professor of Anatomy in Edinburgh, for dissection. (The Murder Act 1752 forbade the burial of anyone executed for murder and bodies were generally sent for dissection, as they were the only legal source of cadavers for medical students at the time, although the

Act also permitted bodies to be left hanging in chains.)

Before she left court Margaret Shuttleworth announced,

> I have no doubt but I will suffer, but I will die innocent of the crime of which you have found me guilty.

Margaret's life seems to have had a certain symmetry to it. She had been born on 20 September 1785; the accident which resulted in the death of the baby at the races happened on the same day in 1796; she had been married on 20 September 1806 and her death warrant was pronounced on that date in 1821.

Today, forensic science would have been able to tell us so much about the killing with blood spatter showing where Shuttleworth had died and even how the blow or blows had been administered – were they delivered by someone right- or left-handed, or was the killer taller than Mrs Shuttleworth?

Curiously enough, Tindal's advocate, Mr Maconochie, had suggested in his closing speech that Henry couldn't have been murdered in the passageway as it was too small to allow blows of the force required to have been delivered there.

Without such evidence proving or disproving her guilt, it is likely that, on the same facts today the case would be found, not proven. No one seemed to know whether the close gate had been locked or not, whether the small poker was the murder weapon or even whether the accused was in a fit state to murder anyone. The accused was not aware that the maid was not at home and the neighbour, Henry Farquharson, and possibly others, were placed at the scene of the crime.

Even the evidence that she was agitated seems harsh given that, if her story was true, she had literally stumbled across the body of her husband.

There were even suggestions of another culprit. Petitioning the Home Secretary for clemency, part of Tindal's plea was that:

> A person of the name of ---- ---- stated that he had been in the neighbourhood of the dwelling-house of the deceased on the night the murder was committed; that he heard noises within the house, and that he went down the entry which was mentioned by other witnesses as having been shut; this person pledged to come forward on your petitioner's trial, but he disappeared in a mysterious manner, after making some very material admissions to his wife in Montrose.

The person named by Margaret Tindal was examined by a Sheriff and 'nothing found against him'. This proof of innocence is why the name was withheld in all later accounts.

The rumours persisted however and, according to the *Montrose Chronicle*, the named individual had come home at about 5:00 am with blood on his hands on the morning of the murder. He had apparently confessed to his wife that he had been in Shuttleworth's house, along with his half-brother, a well known whisky smuggler.

This man then left town for a period but did eventually return, denying the charge against him.

The other petition was, in the words of the *Montrose Review*,

> signed by a number of respectable gentlemen of this town, praying for a commutation of punishment, that the feelings of the inhabitants might be spared the horrible exhibition of a public execution – and that too of a female.

On 6 December a letter was received from Lord Sidmouth in London. It was addressed to Rev P Cushnie, one of the local ministers who had campaigned on behalf of the unfortunate woman but, because he was out of town, it was opened and read out by Provost Gibson, the same medical practitioner who had examined the body earlier. Despite the fact that it was 9:20 pm, a crowd had gathered to hear the Provost read the letter.

The answer was that,

> the case of the prisoner had already received the most minute investigation of the Privy Council, and that the petition contained no grounds upon which His Majesty's [George IV] advisers could feel themselves warranted to recommend the interposition of royal clemency.

Tindal herself felt that her reputation for drinking and her stormy relationship with her husband resulted in her conviction, rather than the strength of the evidence against her.

Still protesting her innocence, Margaret Tindal or Shuttleworth was eventually hanged at Montrose before a crowd of around four thousand people. The crowd would probably have been even larger but, because sentence had been postponed twice as a result of the petitions, many thought that the sentence would not be carried out.

Gallows, hired at a cost of £30, were erected just outside the Tolbooth on the south side of the Town House and reports from the time give a full description of the gibbet.

The scaffold platform was twelve feet square and had been built ten feet above the ground, presumably to give the crowd a good view. At the front of the scaffold was the drop (trapdoor), which was four feet square.

The gibbet itself consisted of two upright posts which stretched eight feet above the scaffold and therefore eighteen feet above the ground. The tops of the posts were connected by a transverse beam with a pulley in the middle and another on one end through which the fatal cord passed and was made fast to a cleat a little below the pulley. The drop was hinged at the back and upheld by another beam at the front which turned on a bolt at one end and was supported by a cord at the other and attached to the gibbet. Immediately the cord was cut, the beam supporting the drop fell by its own weight and the drop turned down on its hinges.

4 *The old tolbooth in Montrose*

Because the execution was to take place so close to the Tolbooth there was no procession as such, although the military had marshalled at the Market Cross at noon and three hundred and sixty special constables gathered in the Guild Hall at 12:30 pm.

As the Steeple bell tolled its doleful message, the assembled multitude felt the full force of the gale and incessant rain but Mrs Shuttleworth sat, apparently unmoved, on the platform.

The assembly sang the 51st psalm before Dr Patterson, minister of the Parish Kirk, led them in prayer. He then put several questions to Margaret, asking if she was guilty of the murder of her late husband or knew anything about his death. She denied any involvement.

Although already pinioned she did her best to shake hands with the

Minister before she addressed the crowd, warning particularly of the evils of excessive drinking.

The noose was put around her neck and a white mask, the means generally used to prevent the crowd viewing the grotesque struggles of the condemned man or woman being strangled, was put over her head. She was given a handkerchief to drop when she felt ready to meet her fate. Her last words were quite clear,

> Lord have mercy on me; Christ have mercy on me; I die an innocent woman. I am innocent of and ignorant of the death of Henry Shuttleworth; I loved my husband as I loved my life. Drinking and threatening words have brought me to my ruin; Jesus Christ receive my soul.

She dropped the handkerchief and the executioner cut the cord with his axe ...

5 *From an image printed in a contemporary broadside about the execution of Margaret Shuttleworth*

The *Review* reported her hanging in some detail, although it also showed a measure of sympathy.

> Never, we believe, was a poor creature in her situation more mis-represented. That you gossiped out and patched up a case on the uncharitable, the horrid, the hanging side of a question, which, with all due respect to the laws of the country, the acknowledged conscientiousness and integrity of the judges and jurors, is still wrapped up in some inexplicable mystery? Let it be distinctly understood, however, that we offer no opinion of her guilt or innocence of the foul crime for which she has to been cut off from the land of the living. This was settled by those whose prerogative it is to judge; and the law has been executed upon her. It is the vindictive spirit that has pursued her, even to the gibbet, that we wish to reprove.

The view that, in our modern terminology, the conviction was unsafe seems to have been widely held and even the Kirk Session of the Parish

Kirk, a difficult body to convince of innocence at the best of times, recorded her death with the comment that she had been sentenced on largely circumstantial evidence.

We may think that we live in a bureaucratic state today but there is, in the *Montrose Tolbooth Book*, a receipt for the body from the College of Edinburgh, signed by Dr Monro's assistant.

What makes this sad tale even worse is that later an Irishman was said to have confessed to the murder of Henry Shuttleworth. According to him, Shuttleworth let him into the house after the servant-girl had left. After a few drinks a quarrel started and the Irishman struck Shuttleworth several times with the poker before leaving it beside Margaret Tindal's bed as she lay in her drunken stupor.

To make his escape he then locked the door from the inside and climbed out through the large chimney.

That said, the report described the Irishman as 'a tramp', whose story couldn't be relied on.

Among the watercolours by Montrose historian J G Low in Angus Council's Museum collection is one of Farquharson's Brewery. The notes alongside relate that 'the site is now occupied by Knox's Church and on ground extending down to the floods mark was a brewery known as Farquharson's Brewery'. Unfortunately the notes are Low's own (he died in 1944) and consequently, somewhat dated, and the site is in fact of the old Knox's Church in Castle Street, which later became a cinema and was then used as a boxing club, before it was demolished and replaced by the Castlegait Surgery.

Ironically, it is now the site of the local Citizen's Advice Bureau where the staff assist the public with legal problems.

On Thursday 20 April 1826 the trial of David Balfour opened at the Circuit Court in Perth. Balfour, a seaman from Dundee, was charged with murder, namely

> That on 21st December last, the prisoner did, within a house in the Murraygate of Dundee, violently attack and assault Margaret Clark, his wife, and did with a butcher's knife inflict a severe wound on her left arm, and on the left breast and side, by the latter of which she was stabbed to the heart, and instantly bereaved of life.

Initially, Balfour entered a plea of Guilty but, after the intervention of his counsel, he reluctantly changed his plea to Not Guilty.

The first witness for the prosecution was David Anderson who acknowledged that he was a lodger in the house in the Murraygate owned by Robert Clark, the father of the deceased. He explained that the house was also occupied by Robert, his sons Andrew and James, and the deceased. Sometimes the accused stayed there too.

Anderson agreed that he was living in the house on the night of the murder and described the circumstances of Mrs Balfour's death. Andrew and James had been at work. The prisoner and his wife had only stayed there for two nights. The house had three rooms and on the first night the couple had shared a room but on the second night they occupied separate rooms as Mrs Balfour had expressed the view that she was afraid to sleep with her husband 'as he was not himself'. The witness simply took this to mean that the prisoner had not been altogether sober.

At about 8:30 in the morning, the witness heard Mrs Balfour twice cry 'murder'. He ran to her room to find her slumped on her knees with blood streaming from her left side. She told him, 'Oh, David, my husband has murdered me!' Just then, her father came into the room but within two minutes she was dead.

Asked what he knew about the other circumstances of the killing the witness said the deceased had told him that her husband was jealous of a man called McLeod, who came from Greenock. McLeod's son was also a resident in the house and the prisoner believed his wife had too much respect for the boy.

The next witness was Robert Clark, the deceased's father, who said his daughter had expressed no fears to him before, although he had suggested going to the police as the prisoner had used threatening language to her the previous night and his general behaviour had been 'outrageous'.

A night-watchman, Mr Clark said he had returned to the house after work on the morning of the murder at around 5:00 am and gone to bed. He was awakened at about 8:00 am by his daughter's scream and he jumped up and ran to her room, just in time to see her fall to the floor. As he lifted her up he looked round the room but saw no one until David Anderson ran in. She died minutes later without saying anything to him.

One of his sons came into the room and found a bloody knife lying near the fire place. The witness identified the knife in court and confirmed that it didn't belong in the house.

Another witness, Margaret Ireland, said she knew the couple. On the night before the murder the accused had come to her house and had a glass. (A large measure, usually of whisky.)

He seemed depressed and worried about something and told her that by the same time the next day he would be in jail. Later that day she was in the deceased's house and heard the accused tell his wife she shouldn't go out the following day.

The witness then suggested to the deceased that she shouldn't stay there but she had replied that she had 'put up with it many a night, and she hoped to God she could put up with another'.

The accused had also offered to tie his wife's shoelace saying to her, 'O, my dear'. When she rebuffed his advances he then told witness, out of earshot of his wife, 'My wife's mad, and is fit for bedlam'.

When he suggested to his wife that they go to bed together she refused him to which he replied, 'O, my dear, can I not regain your heart'. She responded, 'Not tonight'.

Ireland told the court she was a relative of the deceased and that she felt the accused was 'much attached' to his wife. He generally spoke to her in affectionate terms but agreed 'there was something between them she could not understand'.

She had also heard the deceased, whom she described as a respectable character who 'had no evil in her', ask him to stay away from her and she was aware that the accused was jealous of his wife.

Another witness, Thomas Houston, swore that the accused had told him what he proposed to do on the morning of the murder while a subsequent witness, William Small, flesher, identified the accused as the man he had given a knife to that same morning.

A turnkey at the jail in Dundee, Charles Watson, told the court that the accused had come to the jail that morning and demanded to be admitted.

Following the medical evidence the accused's declaration was read out. It detailed the incidents, and particularly his feelings about his wife and McLeod, which had caused serious rifts between the parties and ultimately led to the fatal outcome. He admitted the charge.

Defence counsel, Mr McNiel, made an eloquent plea for clemency, suggesting that the deceased's offhand manner with her husband and her keeping the son of a man he obviously despised in the house against his express wishes, coupled with the way her family treated him, must have resulted in temporary madness in an otherwise affectionate husband. Such actions, he argued, had led, if not to positive insanity, at least to a state where his client had lost all responsibility for his own actions.

He argued that his client had suffered from 'a state of mental delusion' which he believed would permit the jury to return a verdict in terms that suggest that the ultimate penalty was too severe in this instance.

The judge, Lord Pitmilly took the opposite view. He agreed that the members of the jury would no doubt have feelings of sympathy for the accused but he continued

> it would be a most dangerous matter for the country, if the very atrocity of a crime, and the extraordinary and violent manner of its perpetration, were to be entertained as palliations; and here no evidence of insanity, properly, so called, appear.

Nevertheless, after an hour's deliberations the jury, unanimously, found Balfour guilty of murder 'but, by a large majority, recommended mercy'.

His Lordship, who had no option under the law, sentenced Balfour to be executed at Dundee on 2 June and his body sent to Dr Monro for dissection.

A number of appeals for the sentence to be commuted were lodged without success and, as he awaited his execution, Balfour appeared rational and surprisingly resigned to his fate.

Some years before while at sea, Balfour had fallen from the mast of a ship and landed on the deck, a fall that had caused severe head injuries. Whether or not that is what had given rise to his actions we cannot be certain but it will not be the last occasion on which we shall hear similar tales.

Nevertheless, Balfour was more than willing to tell his visitors of his love for his late wife. He had been ready to forgive her except that she was apparently unwilling to give up her association with another man and be content living with him.

On the Wednesday before his execution he saw most of his acquaintances for the last time, including a number of his late wife's relatives with whom he exchanged what a press report of the time referred to as 'expressions of mutual forgiveness'.

His last night on earth was spent apparently peacefully, reading scripture and writing letters. Despite the fact that the sound of the gibbet being built could clearly be heard his only comment was that he was sure the men involved would much rather be employed doing another job.

As Friday 2 June dawned Balfour was joined in his cell by three of the local clergy who spoke and prayed with him at some length. Outside, the mood on the streets was particularly sombre and, as 2:00 pm approached, the shops closed and a strange quietness descended on the neighbourhood, proof it was believed, of the sympathy many felt for the unfortunate Balfour.

Mindful of the possibility of some form of disturbance the magistrates had taken steps to maintain order by having constables mix with the assembled crowd.

The gibbet, platform and drop, which had been erected at one of the windows of the Guild Hall to allow access from inside, was the same apparatus used in the execution of John Watt in 1801.

The magistrates, councillors and commissioners of police all assembled in the Hall where Balfour was pinioned and told that the executioner was present. At that point he appeared very calm and announced,

I am ready and willing; when I am bound by him, I am free. Come forward; don't be afraid; you have no reason.

Then, accompanied by the three ministers and Mr Dick, the prison surgeon, Balfour went down into the Guild Hall where he bowed most respectfully to the assembled company before taking his place on the scaffold at around 2:15 pm.

Aged about forty, Balfour was of medium build and dressed in the dark suit that he had worn at his trial. What was most startling however was his apparent composure. Following the singing of the hymn he had selected, he stepped forward to give the traditional speech permitted to a condemned man.

You will, no doubt, think that my situation is bad, and I admit myself that it is so; yet, awful as it is, I hope for mercy through the blood of my Saviour, and in this alone my hope rests. I hope that you will all take warning by the example of my death, which you are about to witness, and that it may have a proper effect on your minds. I do regret that I have brought so much disgrace upon the town, and dishonour upon God; but I am willing and ready to die for it.

The following words were indistinct, and he bowed slightly before continuing:

My friends, I acknowledge the justice of my sentence, and that it is proper that I should die for what I have done. I have sinned both against God and man, and justly forfeited my life; and had I been in the judge's place, as I am now upon the scaffold, upon myself I would have pronounced the very same sentence.

The Rev Murray had just started to pray in what was described as 'a most impressive manner' when something strange happened. There was an agitation among the crowd which was accompanied by a noise resembling the sound of coach wheels and horses hooves. Just as the sound ended there was a tremendous commotion among the crowd with people being pushed against each other as they tried to move in different directions at once and some were even carried along, helplessly, into nearby side streets. All the time women and children screamed and many people were trodden underfoot.

Spectators watching the proceeding from upstairs windows reported the masses moving like the sea, with spaces suddenly appearing before being filled up again just as quickly.

At the point when the noises had first been heard the magistrates, fearing a rescue attempt, had ordered the doors of the Guild Hall to be locked and the execution to take place without further delay.

Consequently, Mr Murray finished his prayer and Balfour was taken back inside to be prepared for execution. As this was taking place there was another episode just like the initial one but, although there was some further agitation among the crowd, the mass panic didn't reach the previous level.

Balfour was led to the gallows with a white blindfold covering his face and the noose around his neck. As he reached the drop he gave the signal that he was ready and at about 2:45 pm the final act took place. Within a minute he had ceased to struggle, although his body was left suspended for almost an hour before being cut down and taken back into the Hall. It was dispatched to Dr Monro that evening.

It was an execution unlike any other in that the talk among the crowd was not about the execution but about what had caused the mysterious noises and commotions.

There were many readymade theories: it was the work of the Devil; perhaps it had been sparked off by an infuriated ox, a mad dog or a restive horse; others were of the belief that there had been a small earthquake; some took the view that it had somehow been the work of pickpockets, raised to cover their nefarious activities.

Contemporary reports dismiss the idea of a carriage of any kind being in the vicinity, suggesting some simple cause such as the noise made by the feet of some of those present, heard in the pervading silence, having taken on some significance and caused the crowd, who collectively were already in a state of mass excitement, to react.

There were few casualties other than one women with a broken breast bone, although many hats and shoes were lost, or as the report continues – exchanged – 'some for the better, others for the worse'.

1826   Mary Elder or Smith

Mrs Smith was forty-two years old and had lived with her husband David, a well-to-do farmer, at Denside near Monikie for some twenty years.

The couple had four adult children, two boys and two girls. Two servant-girls, Margaret Warden and Jean Norrie, lived-in, and another, Barbara Small, stayed with the foreman and his wife. There were a number of other servants, including sisters Agnes and Ann Gruar, who stayed elsewhere.

Margaret Warden was twenty-four years old and unmarried. Just four years before she had been forced to return to her widowed mother where she had given birth to a child which her mother kept and reared. After a decent interval, Margaret Warden returned to Denside where she resumed her duties much as before.

The family owned three farms and were reasonably prosperous so it is likely that Mary Elder had ambitious plans to see her sons make good marriages. We can therefore imagine her reaction when she discovered in the summer of 1826 that her youngest son, George, and Margaret were not only courting but that Margaret was expecting. As far as Mrs Smith was concerned it was probably bad enough that Margaret was a servant but her previous indiscretion meant that she was certainly not a suitable match for her son.

At least twice poor Margaret was on the receiving end of some moralising from her mistress who no doubt saw her as a scarlet woman intent on leading her son astray. These lectures had upset Margaret so much that she returned home, yet, on each occasion, Elder went to Dundee to make her peace with the girl and convince her she was needed back at Denside.

On the second occasion Mrs Warden walked part of the way back with Elder who told her she wished Margaret wasn't pregnant before remarking that the situation would be 'a trial' for both herself and Margaret's mother.

Elder obviously had a solution in mind however as she then informed Mrs Warden that she was off to Dundee and would 'get something for Margaret there'. It appears likely that, far from accepting the situation, she wanted her at Denside where she would have control over the luckless girl and procure an abortion.

Jean Norrie, the other servant, shared a bed with Margaret in the farm kitchen.

On Tuesday 4 September, Elder had brought through a glass of something for Margaret. She said she had already had some herself and then offered each of the girls a drink and a lump of sugar to take afterwards.

Jean had taken about a teaspoonful and Margaret had drunk the rest. Giving evidence later, Jean couldn't recollect the taste and admitted she hadn't been taken by its whitish appearance. It was not like any castor oil she had ever tasted, more like cream of tartar.

The two girls went to bed about 10:00 pm but the following morning Margaret was extremely sick and Jean took her back to bed. When she returned at lunchtime Margaret was still there and by evening she was extremely ill. At one point Jean had suggested to her that she was dying to which she had replied, 'Some folk would be glad of that'.

On the Thursday morning Margaret was much worse, complaining of 'her inside' and of a great thirst, although anything she drank came up again almost immediately.

Margaret wanted her mother, who lived just two or three miles away, sent for but Elder told her to hold her tongue.

That night Elder asked Margaret if she thought 'a drap whisky would be good for her'. Jean replied that 'she had got enough of that' or something similar. When Elder left the room Margaret had said her inside was burnt with whisky, or that her mistress had burnt it and Jean told her that she ought not to take any more of the drinks offered to her by Elder. This remark would suggest that the witness was aware that harm was being done to Margaret, although she may not have understood exactly what was being administered.

Early on the Friday morning Mrs Warden was finally sent for and she sent a message to Dr Taylor of Broughty Ferry asking him to come to Denside at once.

By this time Margaret was drifting in and out of consciousness. Cholera and typhus were rife in the area and Mrs Warden no doubt thought that her daughter had one of those diseases.

When Dr Taylor arrived at about 1:00 pm, Elder took him into the parlour where she told him of her servant's symptoms but only admitted giving her castor oil. Her excuse for failing to send for a doctor sooner was that the girl was somewhat scatterbrained so she hadn't really taken the matter seriously. Interestingly, she told Taylor that she understood that Margaret was pregnant and asked if the sickness would cause a miscarriage.

The Doctor brought the exchange to an abrupt end to go to Margaret's sick-bed where he found her cold and clammy and with no pulse discernible at either her hands or temple. He tried to speak to her and she managed to tell him she had been sick and purging since Tuesday night.

He quickly realised her condition was hopeless and informed Elder of his findings. She showed little or no emotion but returned to querying the effect of Margaret's continued sickness on her pregnancy, saying that, 'if the gudeman kent it [if her husband knew of the girl's condition] he would be like to tear down the house about them'. She had also said, 'It would be a stain on the family'.

Nevertheless, Dr Taylor left the house believing that Margaret was dying of cholera – he had no reason to think otherwise.

Later, Mrs Warden, Jean Norrie and Ann Gruar were gathered around the bed as Margaret lay dying. She summoned what little strength she had left to call Jean to come closer and, taking hold of her hand said, 'Jean, ye ken wha is the occasion o me lyin here?' 'Ay', replied Jean, 'will you forgie them?' 'Yes', was the reply, 'but they'll get their reward'. When mother and daughter were left alone Mrs Warden asked if anyone had hurt her or given her anything. Her daughter told her, 'Jean Norrie will tell you all about it. My mistress gave me ...' – she was unable to complete the sentence.

She died at nine o'clock that night.

Mrs Warden remained in the house to dress the body and prepare it for burial but nothing was said about the cause of death. Mrs Warden didn't ask any questions and Jean Norrie said nothing.

When Mrs Warden returned home the following day she told her other daughter what Margaret had said but told her to say nothing for the time being.

At Denside, Elder was telling her family that Margaret had died of the fever and, referring to the discolouration of the corpse (it had been dark or black), she said the doctor had said everyone who died of the fever was that colour after death.

She later told Barbara Small that Margaret had, according to Dr Taylor, died of water in the chest.

None of those statements had any truth in them.

Margaret Warden was hastily buried in Murroes churchyard on Sunday 10 September but she wasn't destined to lie there for long. Rumour soon got abroad that the unfortunate Margaret had been poisoned by her mistress in an attempt to prevent her son's 'good' name being brought into disrepute and, just as quickly, the rumours reached the ears of the authorities and the body was exhumed on Saturday 30 September. It was later examined by Drs Johnston and Ramsay of Dundee, with Dr Taylor also in attendance.

The internal organs, which were remarkably well preserved, showed traces of acute inflammation. As a result, further examination of the organs was made before Elder was summoned to appear before the Sheriff at Dundee.

It was argued on her behalf that she was not fit enough to undergo a judicial examination but, after a medical assessment by Dr Johnston, she was declared fit and travelled with her husband, Dr Johnston and one of her sons to meet the Sheriff at Four Mile House, an inn between Denside and Dundee, on 2 October.

There, she denied having spoken to Dr Taylor in the terms he described or knowing that the deceased had been pregnant.

She would only admit to giving the deceased castor oil, bought from a druggist called Mrs Jolly, and some 'lozenge wine' and categorically denied having any access to poison. According to her statement, the men who came to the farm to deal with the rats always brought their own poison and anyway, it had been at least two years since rat catchers had been needed at Denside.

Evidence was given at the trial that Elder, who, despite protesting that she wasn't fit to be examined, had remained remarkably composed throughout until the final question was put to her. Asked if she had any poison she swore that

> she had got no drug or other such article from any other person than Mrs Jolly, on the Friday preceding the death of the girl.

The fact that such a question was asked showed the level of the authority's suspicions and she was imprisoned at Dundee.

Whether a night in prison gave her time to think over what she had said or whether she was warned by others of the authority's lines of inquiry isn't clear but suddenly, the following morning, she requested another examination so that she could tell the truth.

Suddenly, she had remembered that she had purchased 'something' to kill the rats that infested Denside Farm from William Dick, a surgeon in Dundee. Her memory of other matters was suddenly clearer as well – there were rats everywhere at Denside, so many in fact that the farm servants had even complained about the noise they made!

She even insisted Margaret Warden had watched as she mixed the poison with meal as instructed by Mr Dick and stuffed the resulting mixture into holes in the loft above the bothy.

Yet, despite her sudden certainty about the past, she couldn't be sure however that the 'something' she had purchased was poison. She agreed that the packet had writing on it – but she didn't know what it said!

Mary Elder or Smith, wife of David Smith, a farmer at West Denside in the parish of Monifieth, was charged with having

> on the 5th September 1826 ... wilfully, maliciously, and feloniously, administered, or caused to be procured or administered, to Margaret Warden, then servant to David Smith, a quantity of arsenic, or other poisonous substance, mixed up with water, or other liquid, inducing her to swallow the same, by falsely representing to her that it was a medicine intended for her benefit; and she having accordingly swallowed the same deleterious mixture, became immediately thereafter violently ill, and

lingered in great pain until the 8th of the said month, when she died in consequence thereof; she being thus wilfully, maliciously and feloniously Murdered.

The accused entered a plea of Not Guilty.

After several postponements the trial at the High Court of Justiciary in Edinburgh finally got underway on 19 February 1827.

The defence team, which consisted of Francis Jeffrey and Henry, later Lord, Cockburn, two of the ablest advocates at the Scottish bar, lodged several special defences the main thrust of which was that Margaret hadn't been poisoned and that, if she had, then it was self-administered.

Having given the court her version of events, Jean Norrie agreed under cross-examination that the deceased had remarked months before her death she 'would surely do some ill to hersel' but said she hadn't taken the words seriously.

Ann Gruar also told the court that when working in the fields with the deceased she had told her, 'she wad put an ill end to hersel'. This was the first time Ann had mentioned this to anyone, other than to another woman in the field whom she didn't know.

Despite these attempts to suggest suicide, Mrs Smith's version of events seemed particularly flawed.

Tellingly, Dr Dick agreed that he had obtained the poison for the accused, saying the word 'poison' was written on one side of the packet and 'arsenic' on the other.

In addition, none of the farm workers who gave evidence said they had heard rats or made a complaint about them to the accused.

The Smith's own doctor, Dr Alexander, said he had examined the accused on 1 October 1826, the day before her arrest, and found her to be suffering from a nervous attack for which he prescribed antispasmodics. He felt that at that point she wasn't fit to be legally examined and also pointed out that such attacks could lead to memory loss.

Dr Johnston, the doctor who had travelled with the accused to Four Mile House, contradicted this evidence, saying that she had appeared perfectly fit both before and after she had made her declaration.

The medical practitioners, including Dr Taylor who had initially diagnosed cholera as the cause of death, all agreed that there had been arsenic present in the body.

But, and it is a huge but, although it was possible to test for the presence of arsenic at the time it was not until 1836 that an indisputable scientific test, the Marsh test, was devised.

Two doctors, Fyfe and Mackintosh, gave evidence for the defence. Dr Mackintosh argued that the symptoms displayed by the deceased could indicate either cholera or arsenic poisoning but he agreed under cross-examination that Margaret had been poisoned.

It was 11:00 pm before the Lord-Advocate rose to address the jury on behalf of the Crown. His speech left little doubt about guilt – or so it might have seemed.

He argued that there could be no doubt that poor Margaret had been poisoned, so that only left the question of who had administered it?

The evidence from Jean Norrie, the deceased's deathbed conversations with her mother and the testimony of other witnesses all cast doubt on the likelihood of Margaret having committed suicide.

Motive was obvious – Mrs Smith wanted to avoid her family being disgraced. She may simply have intended, initially at least, to procure an abortion but the use of arsenic took the matter to another level.

Jeffrey, on behalf of Mrs Smith, began his address at 1:00 am. (The case had commenced at 9:00 am the previous day.) He put forward the argument that the deceased had died of cholera and proceeded to argue that his client had no motive to kill the deceased before casting doubt on the science involved in the identification of poison.

The Lord Justice Clerk started his charge to the jury at 3:00 am and didn't finish until 5:30 am. The jury having, as was the custom, stood up when the Lord Justice Clerk began, were never invited to sit so that they remained standing for the whole two-and-a-half hours. He accepted that the young woman had been poisoned but reiterated the question – by whom?

By the time his Lordship finished, the jurors had been engaged in the case for some eighteen hours and they must have been relieved to hear that he wished a written verdict to be delivered at 2:00 pm. They returned at the appointed time and delivered a unanimous verdict of Not Proven.

It may have been that the jury were unwilling to convict simply because Mrs Smith would then hang. This was a sentiment which often resulted in guilty verdicts, irrespective of the nature of the murder, being accompanied by requests for clemency. In law, no such course was open to judges but perhaps it made individual members of juries feel better about themselves.

Mrs Smith had to be spirited away as the general, and not unreasonable, belief was that she was guilty.

One example of public feeling is reflected in a popular song of the time:

The Wife o Denside

Ye'll a hae heard o the Wife o Denside,
Ye've surely heard word o the Wife o Denside,
Wha pushioned her maid to keep up her pride
An the devil is sure o the Wife o Denside.

***

The Wife o Denside, the little wee buddie,
She tried to tak up the trade o the howdie [midwife],
But ah! Ha ha! Her skill was but sma,
For she pushioned baith lassie an bairn an a.

***

Her tippet was brown and her veil it was black,
An three lang feathers hung over her back,
Wi her purse by her side fu o guineas sae free,
That saved her frae death at the Cross o Dundee.

***

Oh! Jeffrey, oh! Jeffrey, ye hinna dune fair,
For ye've robbed the gallows o its lawful heir,
An it hadna been you an your great muckle fee,
She'd hae hung like a trout at the Cross o Dundee!

Perhaps the verdict is best summed up however in the words of advocate and novelist Sir Walter Scott when he saw Mrs Smith, who according to Henry Cochrane,

> was guilty, but acquitted, of murder by poison. The case made a great noise. Scott's description of the woman is very correct. She was like a vindictive masculine witch. I remember him sitting within the bar looking at her.

As they were leaving, Sir Walter's remark upon the acquittal was:

> Well sirs! All I can say is, that if that woman was my wife, I should take good care to be my own cook.

6 *St Vigeans kirk and kirkyard*

On a Sunday morning in October 1826 the congregation at St Vigean's Church near Arbroath had just settled down for their usual lengthy helping of fire and brimstone from the pulpit when the sound of digging in the earth outside was heard.

Eventually, a brave soul looked out into the kirkyard to see a group of men gathered around a recently dug grave, obviously intent on exhuming the bodies it contained and, before long, the entire congregation had lost interest in the minister's words of salvation.

Just a few days before, Jane Wishart, a blind, single mother, and her newborn infant, her second child, had been interred in that very grave. Both mother and baby had been gravely ill and died within hours of each other.

Just like the case of Margaret Warden, it wasn't long before it was being widely rumoured that Jane Wishart had been poisoned and, once again, this quickly came to the attention of the authorities who decided that the matter was worthy of investigation. As a result, the decision was taken to exhume the bodies, although for some odd reason this was carried out during morning worship.

On the Monday morning statements were taken from the neighbours and Margaret Wishart was arrested and brought before the Sheriff at

Arbroath where she was detained in the Tolbooth to await further instructions from Crown Counsel.

The case called at the Circuit Court in Perth on 14 April 1827 when Margaret Wishart was charged with having:

administered a quantity of arsenic to her sister Jane Wishart, residing with her in Arbroath, on the 3rd, 4th, 5th, or 6th days of October, 1826, which poison was mixed up with a quantity of porridge or gruel, and given to her to eat, – as also to an infant male child of which the said Jane Wishart had been delivered upon the said 6th October, – in consequence of which poisonous mixture the said Jane Wishart immediately thereafter became violently ill, and lingered in great pain until the 8th day of said month, when she died in consequence thereof.

The accused entered a plea of Not Guilty.

The first witness, David Edwards, had been lodging with the accused at the time of Jane's death. He said that he took meals with the women and could recall Jane being ill but couldn't remember seeing her eating anything.

A regular visitor, Katherine Greig, had come to the house on 3 October but he hadn't seen Jane eating anything then either. (The witness appeared to be evasive in his answers and was warned by the court at that point. Mr Smythe, for the Crown, asked for the witness's evidence to be noted in writing and this was done.)

Jane had complained of being unwell on Tuesday evening, blaming some turnip she had got from the milk-boy. She had later complained of a pain in her bowels but, as far as he knew, she wasn't sick. No one gave her anything at that time, although he was aware of the panel giving her a whisky toddy, he thought on Thursday evening.

He hadn't seen her at all during Friday but when he arrived back that evening he was told she had given birth. The witness said he and the panel sat up with her all night, although he said, because of the position of the bed, he couldn't actually see her.

Jane had told him that Andrew Roy, whom he described as a former lodger, was the father of the child.

The deceased had complained of thirst and Margaret had occasionally given her toast and water from a small stone mug.

The witness went to bed as daylight broke but could still hear the deceased vomiting. He also testified that he saw the child and in fact had it on his knee for most of the night. Charlotte Prophet also had the child for a time and he saw it being sick as well.

The accused had told him she had known of the baby for about a week or two before it was born. In answer to a question from the Judge the witness said that it had been on the Friday night that Margaret had spoken to him about discovering her sister's condition.

She had been surprised and, although she didn't appear angry, she had said it would be

> a great affront to them; nevertheless she said would do the best she could to support the child, and were the mother to die, it would be given out, and she would contribute what she could for its support.

Asked whether the panel appeared to think her sister was going to die he appeared reluctant to answer or was simply unwell but after having had a glass of water said he didn't think so.

Another witness, the aforementioned Katherine Greig, knew both the accused and the deceased. Jane had died on the night of Saturday/Sunday and Greig said she had been in the house on the previous Tuesday between 7:00 and 8:00 pm.

Edwards, the previous witness had been there as well and she saw Jane eating, although she couldn't say whether Margaret ate anything or who had prepared the food. She said Edwards must have seen Jane eating it. There were no plates or spoons for anyone else on the table. Greig described Jane as eating heartily and in good health.

Jane took ill about half-an-hour later, blaming her supper for making her feel unwell. She was put to bed but, because of the position of the bed the witness couldn't see it, she could however hear her retching and vomiting.

The witness left shortly afterwards and it was Thursday before she saw Jane again. She was still in bed, complaining of a general pain and said she had 'been very ill and didn't expect to get better soon'. Greig told the court she didn't see the deceased vomiting on the Thursday.

When she returned to the house at about 9:00 am on Saturday the accused was crying and announced 'oh, there's another child on the way'. Asked when Jane had told her, the accused had replied 'she is delivered' and asked witness to go through to see them.

Jane was too ill to say what was wrong with her, other than telling the witness she was dying.

Margaret's aunt had suggested fetching a doctor for the child who was ill as well but the accused had replied that 'she did not know the use of that', as he wouldn't know what was wrong with the child. Witness felt the panel was aware that mother and child were suffering from the same complaint.

Cross-examined by Mr Pitt Dundas, for the Crown, the witness said she believed 'the panel and her sister lived on good terms'.

The following witness was Jessie Smith or McKenzie, a neighbour of the Wisharts. Margaret Wishart had visited her on a Friday and asked her to come to see Jane. Mrs McKenzie had taken Mrs Prayne, the howdie, along with her but had returned on her own in the evening.

The deceased was complaining of a 'particular drouth' (thirst) but was well enough to talk and she confessed that Andrew Roy was the father of both her 'former child' (the child had died when only a few months old) and this one.

By Saturday morning Jane was very ill and the witness went to fetch Mrs Prayne. The child had also taken ill during the night and the witness described its belly as stiff and hard. The accused said she had given it some gruel and witness then gave it some sugar and water to drink.

Jane had asked for Dr Clark but Margaret had answered,

> I wonder to hear you; for Dr Clark nor all the doctors in Arbroath can do you any good.

The deceased had continued to complain of a raging thirst and the witness gave her water from a dish beside the bed. However anything Jane drank was soon brought up again.

Although the deceased complained of no particular pain she was very restless and died that night. The panel told the witness that before she died, Jane had asked her to keep the child but she hadn't consented.

The child was also very ill and died on the Monday morning.

Cross-examined by Mr Dundas, the witness said she understood that a doctor had seen the child, although she hadn't been there.

Mrs Prayne, the howdie, was the next witness. She explained that she had delivered a male child and had recommended a little warm meat. The panel prepared some water gruel but the deceased had only managed to take a small amount by the time the witness returned later. Jane then agreed to take some tea and Margaret made that for her.

When Mrs Prayne returned in the evening she found the deceased 'rather ill' and vomiting. She asked the howdie to give her something but Mrs Prayne said she couldn't so near her delivery.

Early the following morning, Mrs McKenzie had come for the witness who found the deceased very ill and complaining of thirst.

The witness went to Dr Clark who gave her some mace, a herb which she later infused, and an opium pill. Mrs Prayne gave both the infusion and the pill to the deceased but they were immediately vomited.

She returned at about 10:00 am when she recommended fetching Dr Clark but the panel protested saying,

> everything had been done that could be done – a doctor would do her no good – and she was not able to pay a doctor's charge.

Mrs Prayne then suggested sending for one of their sisters but again the accused protested, saying Jane didn't wish to see any of her relations as they would 'only rail at her'.

The witness returned again in the afternoon when she did what she could for both but without success for the next time she saw them they were being put into a coffin. She had thought the child healthy initially but it too got worse and worse.

Jane's symptoms after the birth had been unlike anything else she had experienced. The panel had suggested she had colic after eating a turnip. This remark was made in the hearing of the deceased who had made no observation about it.

Another resident of the property, Charlotte Prophet, told the court she had lived there for several months. When she first arrived in the house there had been four boarders, one of whom was Andrew Roy.

This witness said that Jane had complained to her about being ill-treated and that she often heard her crying. She had also insisted that she had 'a bad life between her sister and Andrew Roy'.

The witness had regularly seen Andrew Roy and the accused, leaving the house within a few minutes of each other and returning in a similar manner, a pattern which was repeated at least twice per week.

Prophet said the panel had not complained to her of the difficulty of supporting the child.

The following witness was Mary Greig who testified that Jane Wishart had lived with her for a time, although that had been more than three years before.

Jane had admitted to her that her first child, born around that time, was Roy's but had been sworn by her sister and Roy to tell no one. She would have liked to tell her minister so that her other sisters might forgive her but felt bound by her oath.

Greig had met the deceased in Applegate about six months before her death when she pleaded with witness to take her to stay with her, complaining that Andrew Roy 'struck and abused her till she complied with his ways'.

The last time she had met Jane she had told Greig of her latest pregnancy, saying 'her sister would not give her leave to live', and again she pleaded to come and live with the witness.

Greig's next piece of testimony was damning for the defence. She swore that she had visited the accused in prison a number of times and that, on one occasion, the accused had taken her into an empty room in the jail and asked her to say that she had gone with the deceased to Croll's shop to buy poison. Greig had replied that she couldn't say that.

Under cross-examination, Greig said that it was the second time she visited the accused in jail that she was asked to say that she had gone with Jane to buy the poison in Croll's shop. The panel had pleaded with her and, although she had initially been reluctant, she eventually uttered the words in front of a number of prisoners – 'not being on oath she thought there was little harm'.

Bell Sands or Cargill swore to the court that she had been in Margaret Wishart's house after the child was born and saw panel giving the baby something out of a saucer – something like ale barm (yeast). The accused's reaction when she realised she had been seen was unusual and stayed with her for a time – she described her as looking 'as if she had been surprised in a bad act'.

She said the panel,

> used very harsh expressions about her sister and expressed no sorrow about her distress.

There followed an interesting piece of evidence from C Finlay, surgeon, who attended the house. He said the panel showed no

> particular anxiety about the child, nor desired him to do anything for it.

She did however ask him to look at Jane's body but he declined.

The medical evidence was given by Dr Arnot who said he knew the deceased by sight. He, along with Drs Palmer and Sharpey, had attended St Vigean's churchyard when the coffin of mother and child was disinterred. The body was then taken to the schoolhouse and the stomach and other intestines examined.

The stomach was divided into two; one half was retained and the other sent by the mail coach to Dr Christison, professor of medical jurisprudence at Edinburgh.

The witness then read from a 'most minute and scientific report' of the various tests the samples had been subjected to. The conclusions were that the deceased died in consequence of arsenic having been administered – and that at an earlier period than the Friday before her death.

From the appearance (of the samples), and from the evidence he had heard, he was of the opinion the arsenic had been administered on Tuesday.

Dr Sharpey confirmed this evidence.

Professor Christison read his scientific report on the experiments and tests carried on the part of the stomach sent to him and said he concluded that 'death had been occasioned by poison'. He had found one-fortieth-part of a grain of arsenic in the stomach. (The amount is minute.)

Cross-examined, he admitted that 'all the symptoms might appear in natural disease'.

That brought the Crown case to an end.

The panel's declaration was read. Part of this was the assertion that she thought she gave her sister supper on Tuesday 3 October and that Jane partially recovered from her illness as she got up and did some spinning before she was overtaken by the pains of child-labour.

The first witness, David Edward, was committed to jail to await trial for perjury.

Elizabeth McPherson gave evidence on behalf of the accused, saying that she had been in Arbroath prison. She testified that a woman called Mary Greig came to the prison one day, although she couldn't recollect when.

According to the witness, Greig said

had she had been called when the lave [the rest] were called, Margaret Wishart wouldn't have been in jail.

Greig returned the following Monday and witness heard her say that she had gone with Jane Wishart, the blind woman, to several doctors' shops seeking something – she thinks she called it 'bitter apple' – but did not get what they wanted there and finally got it in Croll's.

Mary Mowat or McPherson, mother of the previous witness, corroborated what her daughter had said, other than stating that instead of bitter apple it was arsenic that had been procured at Dr Croll's.

Under cross-examination she agreed that her daughter must have heard what was said.

The court then heard from the jailor, Andrew Durward. He confirmed that Greig had said that she went with the deceased to Dr Croll's, having already tried two other places, and got arsenic there. Durward sent her to Mr Smith, the Procurator Fiscal to give a statement.

The Lord Justice Clerk reprimanded Durward, pointing out that obtaining evidence was not his responsibility.

The final witness was William Ogg who had been jailed for civil debt. He confirmed the previous evidence about where and how the arsenic had been procured.

Mr Pitt Dundas then addressed the jury, bringing out various points that he believed pointed to the panel's guilt before the defence representative, the Honourable Leslie Melville, responded 'with great ingenuity and at considerable length'.

After the Lord Justice Clerk had summed up the members of the jury retired to consider their verdict but were absent for only a short time before they returned having found the accused Guilty, by a majority, of the murder of her sister. They found the case against the accused in respect of the charge of murdering the child Not Proven.

In fact there is another possibility, so obvious that the defence might have ignored it, or perhaps they were simply unaware of it. We have previously seen that arsenic was sometimes taken as a tonic or to improve skin but by 1809 a patent medicine, known as Fowler's Solution, had come onto the market.

The solution, a patent medicine sold as a tonic, was seen as a treatment for virtually every ailment and was reputed to cure everything from lumbago to syphilis. What makes early arsenic poisoning cases difficult is that one of the principle ingredients of Fowler's Solution was arsenic trioxide and the recommended dosage, twelve drops, taken in a glass of water or wine, three times a day for a week, delivered over 100 milligrams of arsenic into the body over that period. (A dose of 250mg would normally be fatal.)

Some people took it over much longer periods and no doubt some increased the dose in the mistaken belief that that would be even more effective. Patients taking Fowler's Solution over a long period would have experienced the problems described earlier and had an increased risk of cancer yet it continued to be prescribed up until the 1950s.

Another difficulty was the fact arsenic was present in all sorts of things, including, in exceedingly small amounts, the human body. In nature, arsenic is found in seaweed and in certain types of fern.

Perhaps more dangerously, during the eighteenth and nineteenth centuries, it was present in many everyday objects such as paints, dyes and even wallpaper, leading to the theory that Napoleon was poisoned by his wallpaper on St Helena. The use of arsenic to develop certain paints which were used in commonplace items, including soaps, toys, candles and soft furnishings, sometimes had tragic results.

Anyway, it is possible that Fowler's Solution or some other such medicine had been taken by the unfortunate Jane or the symptoms exhibited by the deceased could simply have been due to chronic food poisoning or a ruptured gastric ulcer.

Of course, if Jane had been deliberately poisoned and it was not given to her by her sister then it could only have been self-administered. Sadly for Margaret Wishart, the 'evidence' that Jane had purchased the poison herself was too easily dismissed due to the background of the defence witnesses, most of whom were inmates at the jail.

But did Jane Wishart want to end it all? – it seems unlikely.

There was certainly reasonable doubt as to whether a murder had even taken place and, even if it had, whether or not the luckless Margaret was guilty. The jury however were obviously unwilling to consider whether any arsenic in Jane's body might have been self-administered or given as a treatment for her frailty.

7 *The old tolbooth in Forfar*

8 *Margaret Wishart's house in Orchard Street, Arbroath*

Having been found guilty, Margaret Wishart was sentenced to death and she was transferred to the Tolbooth in Forfar where the sentence was to be carried out.

The account of Margaret Wishart's trial and execution in *Tales and Legends of Forfarshire* by Alexander Lowson gives a rather different background to the affair, although where his information comes from isn't clear.

He writes that Margaret Wishart was generally thought of as a decent but poor young woman, who had been in the service of Provost Webster of Forfar for some five or six years, before returning to Arbroath to look after Jane when their mother died. (Lowson refers to her throughout as Jean.)

On her return to Arbroath, Margaret had rented a house in Orchard Street where she made a meagre living from having four lodgers, one of whom was Andrew Roy, and by occasionally taking in washing.

Lowson describes Andrew Roy as her 'young man', and says he visited her regularly when she lived and worked in Forfar but did not appear to be in any rush to make an 'honest woman' of her.

Some eighteen months after she started her new venture her life suddenly changed. Roy, a regular churchgoer and a fine tradesman with his own business, appeared to be an upright citizen and was well thought of in the town. Yet, whatever Margaret's understanding of their relationship might have been, Andrew obviously had other ideas as in September 1826 he had sold up and apparently emigrated to America.

After the deaths, there were many know-alls who

> werna not at a' surprised; they aye thocht there was something wrang an that it was easy seen that Jane/Jean Wishart an Andrew Roy were ower thrang [intimately associated].

Ironically, the death warrant was sent to Provost Webster, Margaret's former employer, who had the unpleasant duty of reading it out to a meeting of the Town Council on 28 April.

The Provost told his fellow councillors that many people were convinced of Margaret's innocence and felt that the evidence against her was entirely circumstantial. A petition seeking mercy had already been sent to the King from the authorities in Perth and he proposed that the Forfar Town Council should follow suit. His recommendation was unanimously agreed.

Clemency was not recommended and consequently there was no stay of execution, although in the end, the execution was delayed until 16 June due to Margaret Wishart's mental state. Unsurprisingly, Forfar had no hangman and Thomas Williams, the Edinburgh hangman, agreed to carry out the deed for a fee of ten guineas (£10.50) plus three guineas (£3.15) travelling expenses.

Just the day before the execution, a large space on the street, including the Town House itself, was enclosed and the scaffold erected beside the east window of that building.

On the morning of her execution Margaret requested that the jailer and his family take breakfast with her; which they did.

Thousands gathered, on a sunny Saturday afternoon, to see the final act of this long-running tragedy, although the crowd was not as large as anticipated despite the fact that there had been no execution in Forfar since the hanging of Andrew Low in 1785.

The execution itself followed the usual pattern with several clergymen attending the condemned woman in the weeks before and on the day. At 2:00 pm her irons were removed and, when the executioner was introduced to her, she rose to her feet and shook hands with him.

In the Town Hall she thanked all who had 'any concern with her' for their kindness before a shortened version of the 51st psalm was sung.

The official party moved onto the scaffold where the rope was placed around her neck and the cap placed over her face.

Despite her situation, Margaret Wishart seemed remarkably composed and she spent half-an-hour on the scaffold asking for God's mercy and acknowledging her 'sins and weaknesses' but declaring her innocence of the crime for which she was about to be punished.

Told her time had expired she replied, 'Two or three minutes longer will finish my labour'.

At twenty minutes after three in the afternoon Margaret Wishart signalled that she was ready and within minutes it was all over.

As was the custom of the time, the body was conveyed to the Professor of Anatomy at Edinburgh University to be used in medical research.

9 *Osnaburg Street in Forfar. The pend is at the far end*

Lowson was convinced of Margaret's innocence and he introduced another possible culprit, although it seems unlikely that the man he blamed could have played any direct role in the events.

The owner of the alehouse in the Osnaburg pend, a Mrs Petrie, said there was something 'no usual' about the man who frequented her establishment on the day before the execution. He would speak only to order his drink and then sit for no longer than five minutes at a time, always appearing to be 'restless and nervous'.

He would appear from different directions but, according to Lowson's account,

> the spot on which they were erecting the gibbet might be compared to the candle round which this human moth was flickering.

About three weeks after the hanging, some boys fishing on Forfar Loch spotted what they initially thought was a bundle of old clothes. Pulling the bundle to the shore they were horrified to find that it was a body, so badly decomposed as to be unrecognisable.

No identification was ever made and the body was laid to rest. Lowson remained convinced that the corpse was Andrew Roy, 'the arch-fiend and prime mover' in the tragedy that ended the lives of both Jane and Margaret Wishart.

1833 Enos or Innes Kelley

Kelley, a sailor from Dundee, was charged with the murder of his wife, Janet Mitchell or Kelley, but the wording of the indictment proved fatal to the Crown's case.

The charge against Kelley was that he

> did murder his wife, in so far as you, on 17th August 1833, in your house at Hawkhill, Dundee, wickedly, maliciously, and feloniously, attacked and assaulted the said Janet Mitchell otherwise Kelley, and did with your fists, and with a poker, or with some other weapon to the Prosecutor unknown, inflict one or more wounds on the head, and other parts the person of the said Janet Mitchell otherwise Kelley, and did violently throw or knock her down to the ground, and with your hands and knees did violently press her body to the ground; by all which the said Janet Mitchell otherwise Kelley, was severely and mortally injured; and in consequence of which injuries she immediately or shortly thereafter died, and was thus murdered by you the said Enos or Innes Kelley.

The accused pled Not Guilty and lodged written defences and alleged provocation and self defence.

A neighbour, Margaret Kay, testified that she had seen the deceased the day before the murder and that she seemed to be in good health. At around eleven o'clock that night, the accused, whom she said was 'quite drunk', had come to her house asking for a smoke. She told him she had no tobacco and he left.

Kay heard him go upstairs and waken his wife. The ceiling was thin enough for her to hear everything and she told the court that she then heard Kelley saying, 'Jenny, Jenny'. The deceased had replied, 'If you say I'm drunk you must go out of here, take everything you have and go'. Despite that, the witness said the only other sound she heard was the accused's feet on the floor.

Fearing that there would be 'a scuffle', the witness ran to the deceased's sister's house and told her Kelley 'was fu and wakening Janet'. She had been there for about ten minutes when her son came in, saying Innes was knocking and calling out.

She ran to the house where she found the deceased on her knees with her left leg stretched out full length. Describing the scene, she said the deceased's chin was resting on her breast, her eyes, although half shut, looked fixed and glazed. She was speechless, with a warm foam coming from her mouth.

The accused asked witness to help him lift his wife onto the bed. She didn't think anything untoward about the incident as the deceased suffered from fainting fits and she had helped her onto the bed before. As far as she could tell the deceased seemed 'well enough', although the accused refused to let her do anymore.

The witness left the house and went to another neighbour's, Mrs Edwards, and told her deceased looked 'as like a corpse as she ever saw'. She then went and told the deceased's sister, Susan Hood, and a number of others the same.

Concerned about the deceased, she returned about ten or fifteen minutes later and found the accused sitting in the dark. She offered to light the lamp but as she moved forward the accused ran in front of her and said his wife was 'lying well enough'.

At around four in the morning, the accused knocked and when she went upstairs she found the deceased 'quite dead'. She had blood coming from her mouth and the accused was in 'a greetin manner'.

The witness ran to Mrs Edwards's and then to Susan Hood's and told them Janet was dead. The two women, accompanied by Mrs Duncan, a local midwife, went back to the house with the witness.

It was Mrs Duncan who suggested calling the medical men. The corpse was purple and discoloured, particularly on the side it was lying on and there were purple marks on the back and face. The accused remained standing at the other side of the room throughout. One witness looked for the poker that was kept in the house but couldn't see it.

The witness confirmed that the deceased regularly took fainting fits.

Cross-examined by the advocate for Kelley, the witness agreed that when she offered to light the lamp the accused hadn't objected and that he had gone to the bed and produced the poker to attend to the fire.

Another witness, Charlotte Ogilvie or Mitchell, who lived in the flat below Kelley and his wife, said that on the previous night she had heard the deceased tell the accused that he had ruined her and her family. This was followed by a scuffle that lasted about two minutes before she heard what sounded like a heavy fall, hard enough to make the windows rattle.

She subsequently heard crockery being broken and then three thumps. After about four minutes of silence the witness heard a noise as if something was being dragged across the floor. The witness agreed that the pair often quarrelled and that they abused each other.

Mrs Duncan confirmed the earlier evidence about the state of the corpse and said she believed the deceased had been choked or strangled, probably about three or four hours earlier.

Dr Crichton said he had inspected the body on 18 August and he confirmed that death had been caused by violence and that although the effusion of blood might have had other causes, he stood by his opinion.

However the second medical witness, Dr Webster, told the court he felt the position of the arms was unnatural. That said, he didn't feel that death had been caused by the external blows but possibly by closing the mouth and nose.

The accused's statement was read to the court. In it, Kelley admitted pushing his wife after she got out of bed and that she fell over and couldn't get up again. The downstairs' neighbour, Margaret Kay, had come up and helped him to get her back into bed. His evidence was that his wife had grabbed the poker when she got out of bed but it had fallen from her grasp when she fell.

When he awoke later, sometime between 4:00 and 5:00 am, he found his wife cold and raised the alarm.

Dr Webster's evidence was a disaster as far as the Crown was concerned and before the start of the defence case, the trial judge, Lord Meadowbank, told the jury it was his duty to point out to them that if they believed that death had been as a result of suffocation or pressure applied to the mouth or neck then, in terms of the indictment, 'it would not be safe for them to convict'.

The only defence witness, a fellow seaman called Edward Newall, told the court that he had known the accused since he was a boy and that he was industrious and generally thought to be of good character.

Following the closing speeches, the jury found the charge in the indictment Not Proven 'by a plurality of voices'.

> Lord Meadowbank concurred, and then addressed the prisoner in the most forcible terms – told him that it was an ambiguity in the indictment which had induced the jury to acquit him, while they could have had no doubt of his guilt; and that as it was, he had to depart from this bar with the mark of crime upon his forehead.

1835 Mark Devlin

Mark Devlin was not a murderer. His crime was that he had raped a fourteen-year-old girl and he was tried, found guilty and sentenced to death at the Circuit Court in Perth in May 1835. As was common practice at the time the public were excluded from the court because it was a rape case.

Devlin had been born in County Tyrone in Ireland and had come to Scotland some five years before. Aged twenty-five, he had at least a basic education and so could read and write.

Before his execution, Devlin appeared to realise the terrible nature of his crime and he took refuge in religion. He was however keen to have visitors and seemed relatively at ease, answering any questions put to him. On the day prior to his execution he elected to see only his wife, the minister and the priest, who had been charged with seeing to his spiritual needs, and an Irish friend.

At around one o'clock on the morning of the execution, the silence was broken by the noise of the joiners erecting the gibbet but this seemed to have no effect on Devlin who slept through most of the noise.

A contemporary report of the events of that day, Saturday 30 May, simply relates that when he was visited by the minister and the priest he accepted his fate and hoped for pardon from his Saviour and thanked God that he had been stopped in the midst of his career of crime.

> He died almost without a struggle – a few slight convulsive movements of the body only indicating that life was not extinct.

Those few words fail to give any indication of the drama that had unfolded before and during the execution of Devlin.

For some unknown reason, the executioner either failed to arrive or simply refused to carry out his grisly task, a problem which left the authorities in some difficulty as, in the absence of an official executioner, the duty fell to the newest bailie on the council. One can imagine that the councillor concerned would not have been particularly enthusiastic about the role so that when a volunteer offered to perform the hanging, provided the magistrates allowed him to wear a mask, they accepted.

If the report of the hanging was correct then the man in the mask, whoever he was, seems to have performed his work well.

Needless to say, there was much speculation about the identity of the executioner and rumour became rife that a man called James Livingston, a travelling showman, was the man who had taken on the role.

The rumour became so widespread that Livingston eventually wrote to the *Dundee Advertiser* denying that he had had any part in the proceedings. His letter, published on 5 June, read:

> Sir, You and the public are well aware that the individual who acted as hangman at the execution of Mark Devlin did so in disguise. Some malicious enemy of mine has circulated a report that I was the individual; and I have been openly assailed most opprobiously with the false accusation.
>
> On the day of the execution I was in Forfar market, during the whole day, attending on my hobby-horses; for the proof of this I appeal to the responsible Provost of that borough, Mr Meffan, who granted me permission to exhibit, and to Mr John Stewart, Town Officer, who has sole charge of pointing out the stands on market days; as also to the public of Forfar in general. Perhaps I have not any right to call upon the Magistrates of Dundee for the name of the individual; but I publicly call upon the presiding Magistrate to exonerate me. I am a poor man with a family, and cannot afford to lose my character in such a manner. Trusting

you will give this a corner in your columns – I remain, Sir, your obedient servant, James Livingstone

We, the Magistrates of Forfar, do hereby certify that James Livingstone, from Dundee, was in the Market-place here, from ten o'clock forenoon till eight o'clock evening, of Saturday, the 30th of May last. – Witness our hands at Forfar, the fourth day of June 1835.

Pat Meffan, Provost
John Lawson, Bailie
John Boath, Junior Bailie

The Dundee Magistrates were less forthcoming. Although obviously aware of the man's identity no one, not even many years later, by which time the mysterious executioner was believed to be dead, ever revealed his name.

Devlin was buried within the prison, the Anatomy Act of 1832 having brought to an end the practice of using only the bodies of executed murderers for medical research, the situation that had given rise to grave robbers and murderers such as Burke and Hare.

1835   Alexander Marshall

Alexander Marshall was charged
> for having, on 13th April 1835, murdered his wife, Ann Miller, by stuffing her mouth with tow [flax or jute fibre], and with his hands, squeezing her mouth and throat, thus producing death.

The case seemed to have captured the public imagination and there were few vacant spaces as the short, badly dressed figure of Marshall, a man in his sixties who lived in Chapelshade, Dundee, took his place in the dock. There he fumbled with a piece of paper throughout the trial which lasted from 11:00 am until 7:30 pm.

A neighbour, Mrs Oudney, told the court she lived 'butt and ben' from Marshall, so close that their doors touched when they were both open. She confirmed that Ann Miller had been in very poor health.

She had seen Miller at about 1:30 pm on the day of her death at another neighbour's, Mrs Roger's. The deceased had apparently gone there to get a needle threaded but had forgotten to take the needle and thread with her.

Mrs Oudney saw Miller later in the day when the deceased asked her to 'tie her mutch' (a hood or cap), as she was unable to do so herself. That was the last time the witness saw the deceased.

She told the court that she heard the accused going into his own house at exactly 5:00 pm as the clock struck at the same time. At 6:30 pm she heard him go into Mrs Roger's house and cry out, 'Is Annie there?' Mrs Roger had followed him back to his own house. The witness and her husband also followed and she heard him say, 'Here she is, but she's gone'. When they got into the house they saw the deceased cradling his wife in his arms. At the back of the bed was a poke or bag full of shavings.

Mrs Oudney called to her husband to help her lay the body out on the bed. It was when she lit a candle that she saw the deceased's face properly and noticed some tow sticking out her mouth. At first, she thought it was the deceased's own hair but, on realising what it was cried out, 'Lord Almighty! Such a scene; the woman's choked with tow!' She pulled out the tow and flung it away. The witness said she looked for it later but couldn't find it.

According to her evidence the prisoner then announced, 'Poor thing! I wish I had died for you; but fouks are aye wise behint the hand'.

The accused had said nothing about how she had died but simply went out, obviously in a state of denial, saying he would get a doctor to come and bleed her. He was arrested the following day.

Mrs Oudney didn't go to the Marshall's house again until several days later when she went to collect some clothes to send up to the jail for the accused. She went along with Mrs Reid and a few others. They were tidying up the bed when a 'pickle tow' fell at Mrs Reid's feet. The witness identified a small bunch of tow, about the size of a child's hand, shown to the court.

At that point there was a commotion in the courtroom when the prisoner was spotted trying to drink something from a small phial. The phial, which was later found to contain laudanum, was wrenched from his grasp by a court official and the accused was taken away and his stomach pumped. He had only taken a small amount and he apparently used it regularly.

After a delay of some twenty minutes Mrs Oudney resumed giving evidence. She explained that she had been a frequent visitor to the deceased's house and was aware that the couple didn't get along. She had often heard the prisoner swearing at his wife and she knew he had been violent towards her on a number of occasions.

Cross-examined by Mr A S Cook for the defence she agreed that the deceased had been very feeble, often had to be helped up if she fell and that sometimes she was unable to rise or turn herself in her bed.

Mrs Oudney also confirmed that the prisoner was addicted to drink, although she couldn't say if he was under the influence of any stimulant that night. She was however aware that he took laudanum.

Dr Arrott confirmed that he and Dr Cochrane had inspected the body of the deceased. He believed that death had been as a result of strangulation as there were no visible signs of violence. The blood vessels on one side of the throat had been ruptured however which he said could only have happened before death.

He told the court he had

> never heard of a case where a man was tried for the murder of his wife where there were no external marks of violence about the body.

In this case there were no marks of inflammation or rubbing in the interior of the mouth.

Questioned further by the Crown he agreed that if the tow had been pushed back far enough to cause suffocation he would not expect to find any marks. He also confirmed that he had never come across a case whereby tow pushed down someone's throat had caused strangulation. Nevertheless, he was convinced that in this case death had been caused by some form of external violence, although there were no outward signs of such behaviour.

He agreed that he didn't believe the tow could have lodged in the throat by accident but he appeared to take the view that the tow in the deceased's mouth had not been the cause of death.

No evidence was led by the defence.

Following the closing speeches the jury retired for around an hour before returning to advise that they had found the accused Guilty.

The trial Judge, Lord Medwyn, sentenced the prisoner to be hanged at Dundee on Saturday 24 October.

Although the jury made no recommendation for clemency, a common reaction where the death penalty was involved, Marshall appealed to the Home Secretary and the sentence was respited.

After a delay which involved postponement of the execution, a letter from the Home Secretary's department, dated 30 October, advised:

> I am directed to acquaint you, that, after mature consideration of all the circumstances, his Lordship has felt warranted in advising the extension of the royal mercy, so far as to spare the prisoner's life.

The letter gives no indication of the final outcome although in fact

Marshall's sentence was commuted to imprisonment and transportation.

The whole trial appears to have been unsatisfactory, particularly with regard to the medical evidence about the cause of death which seems to have been confused to say the least.

Of course no such plea would have been recognised then, it may have been that, given the evidence that Mrs Marshall went to get her needle threaded but forgot to take the these items with her, she might have had what we would now term dementia and her behaviour had become too much for Marshall. While this wouldn't excuse Marshall's actions it might, at least in part, have gone some way to explaining what he did.

1838   Arthur Wood

At around half-past one on the morning of Sunday 5 August 1838, Duncan McNab, a night-watchman with Dundee Police, was patrolling near Thorter Row in the city, when he heard noises from one of the houses, as if the residents were fighting. He put it down to the inhabitants being drunk and, as no one was complaining, he simply ignored it!

When he returned to the spot some twenty minutes later he saw a body lying face down in the court, close to the stair leading to the house where Arthur and Henrietta Wood lived.

The body was lying almost straight, although the knees were slightly bent, with its head outwards and feet towards the flight of seven or eight stairs up to the house, immediately below the plattie or platform. The stairs and landing were bounded by a handrail, almost three feet high.

Initially, the witness thought that he was dealing with a drunk but when he touched the body he realised that the man was dead.

McNab left a passer-by, a tailor called Annal, with the corpse while he went to report his grisly find. Following his second visit to the office, a Sergeant Low arrived with a barrow and McNab helped him load the body and take it to the police office.

Low had recognised the deceased as John Drew Wood, the pedlar son of the Woods, and he went to the house to speak to the family.

Arthur Wood and Henrietta Young or Wood, both from Dundee, appeared at the High Court of Justiciary in Edinburgh on Monday 25 February 1839, charged with the murder of their son on the night of 4/ 5 August the previous year.

Henrietta Wood had given birth in December which had prevented the case being heard in the Circuit Court.

The pair were alleged to have murdered their son by dashing or throwing him upon the floor or ground, striking his head on the floor, furniture or some other hard substance and violently twisting a rope or other ligature around his neck whereby his skull was fractured and he was strangled and immediately, or soon thereafter, died and was thus murdered.

Both entered pleas of Not Guilty.

The first witness at the trial was Duncan McNab who confirmed what he had seen and told the court that earlier on the same night he had seen a man, similar to the deceased, knocking on the Wood's door but hadn't seen whether he was admitted or not. He thought the man might have come from Summer's, a nearby public house.

Following McNab, the tailor, William Annal, gave his evidence. He had been drinking in another public house in the area and had left sometime between 1:00 and 2:00 am. He saw McNab with the body and together they had examined the deceased. There was no pulse, although he was able to confirm that the body was still warm.

Sergeant Low confirmed that he had been told of the incident by McNab and had then gone to the scene to arrange for the removal of the body. He confirmed that he had identified the deceased and then gone to the accused's house.

He knocked on the door and, after being asked who was there, was eventually admitted by Arthur Wood who was fully dressed and wearing a white hat but no coat.

Low asked accused if he knew where his son was and was told, 'He didn't know, he is not here and he shan't be here'. At that point Wood turned to his wife and asked if she knew where John was. She answered that she didn't know.

He then asked when she had last seen him and the witness thought she said that he had been at the door around half an hour before but his father wouldn't let him in.

Pushed as to her son's whereabouts she again replied that she didn't know but thought perhaps she had heard him fall over the stair.

Sergeant Low had then asked Wood if he knew about his son falling over the stair. Low thought the male accused replied, 'It wis na me that did it', or something similar.

At that point the body had been removed and an officer left in charge of the prisoners. Low had returned to the police office where the body was examined, in his presence, by Dr Webster, probably around 2:30 am.

The next witness, Mrs Scott, was a neighbour of the Wood family. She agreed that she knew the deceased whom she believed to be about twenty-one or twenty-two. About a week before the death she had heard the family quarrelling and Mrs Wood stamping her foot before ordering her son out of the house.

This was met with a torrent of bad language from the deceased and he had responded that the house was his father's as well as her's. At that point Mr Wood had said he would put an end to his son's existence.

On the night in question the witness had come down the stairs at about half-past midnight and saw John Wood standing in Summer's pub. Later, she saw him going towards his father's house and formed the opinion that he was drunk.

After that she returned to her own house, which faced the Wood's house, and went to bed. As she lay awake, she heard noises which made her get up and look out of her window.

It was at that point, she told the court, that she heard more noises coming from the Wood's house. She thought she heard 'murder' called out very softly and then the deceased saying, 'Don't choke me father'. There were other noises too, like chairs and tables being dragged about and another noise, like someone's head knocking against the floor.

In reply to the 'don't choke me' remark she heard Arthur Wood say, 'I'll be your butcher before you sleep'.

After that she heard Mrs Wood's voice but couldn't make out what she said. The noises stopped at around 1:30 am but Mrs Scott, obviously fascinated by the goings on, remained at the window.

Just as she heard the half-hour strike she saw the Wood's door open and Mrs Wood looked out before the two accused came out carrying the limp form of their son. They carried him to the bottom of the stairs and laid him out on the ground with his feet towards the stairs.

As they climbed the stairs she thought she heard Mrs Wood say, 'We won't be fashed [bothered] again'.

She agreed that she had initially thought that the deceased was simply drunk and that it was only when her husband told her of the murder that she realised the importance of what she had seen.

Dr Webster was next to appear and he explained that he had examined the body which was still warm. From his examination he concluded that the deceased had been the victim of violence. He had suffered a fracture to the skull and strangulation, either of which would have been sufficient to cause death.

The marks around the victim's neck had been caused by a ligature and he had found a small rope in the house which corresponded to these marks. He believed that strangulation was the most likely cause of death, although the skull fracture must have been caused while the victim was in life. The fracture would have rendered the victim insensible however.

His conclusions were confirmed by another witness, surgeon Adam Moon.

Finally, the prisoners' declarations were read. Arthur Wood had sworn the deceased hadn't been at the house on the night of his death while Henrietta Wood agreed that he had been there but that she had refused him admission.

Following the closing speeches and summing up by Lord Moncrieff the jury retired to consider their verdict.

Despite His Lordship's view that strangulation could not have been effected without the cooperation of two persons, the jury, after deliberating for around half-an-hour, found Arthur Wood Guilty by a majority of fourteen to one and the case against Henrietta Wood Not Proven by a simple majority.

Arthur Wood was sentenced to be hanged at Dundee on 18 March.

Wood, who spoke with a strong Irish accent and also had a remarkable resemblance to Burke of Burke and Hare infamy, continued to protest his innocence. Addressing the court after sentencing he said:

> My Lord, may I be permitted to say a few words. I hope neither the honourable judges, magistrates, nor jury, will take amiss what I mean to say. From the manner I have conducted myself this day, I wish to stand for my perfect innocence. I never so much as imagined the commission of the crime, and I hope God will pardon all my crimes. It is because I am innocent that I now stand so boldly forward.

A petition for clemency was got up but all it did was postpone the inevitable for a period of one week.

The condemned man had held out no hope of a commutation of his sentence and in that he was correct. Despite that, he apparently passed the last weeks of his life with firmness and fortitude.

On being told that his appeal had failed he stated calmly that had he been offered a free pardon he might have hesitated in accepting it as he feared he might have returned to his former habits and 'abandoned life'.

He continued to deny all knowledge of the crime, although he admitted that his memory was dulled by alcohol so that when sober he couldn't recall past events. Against that, it has to be said that when apprehended Wood hadn't appeared to be particularly under the influence.

The scaffold, erected outside the Bridewell (gaol), had been completed in the early hours of the morning of Monday 25 March 1839 and the various dignitaries and officials had arrived at about 7:00 am. At the same time, the special constables and one hundred shore porters assembled and the Fire Brigade guarded the doors to the Gaol.

A publication called *The True Scotsman*, which had hinted at a possible disturbance, had been widely circulated in the city and so a detachment of the 1st Royals had arrived to reinforce the local regiment which had been charged with maintaining order. In the event neither was required.

For at least an hour before the time of the execution crowds had been gathering and the square in front of the Bridewell was soon packed with spectators.

At exactly 8:00 am Wood walked calmly onto the platform and after praying addressed the crowd.

> Good people, all of you that look at me this day, take my fate as an example of evil habits, and especially of the common practice of getting drunk, and being disorderly on Saturday nights or Sunday mornings. Remember this. Let it sink into your hearts. I come forward before a just God, to suffer for the sins done in the body; but for the crime I have to suffer for, I know neither art nor part of it – it never entered into my bosom nor my companion's – I never entertained a thought of it, and I die free of any knowledge of it. It has been likewise stated that my wife was the instigator of quarrels between my family and me – this I protest before God never to have been the case. I again return thanks to the Magistrates for their kindness towards me, and beg you to remember that they are placed over you by God, and recollect their laws and instructions, for they are kind to you as fathers; and they have been much more so to me.

After finishing his address he walked towards the drop, the handkerchief signalling his readiness fell from his grasp and the bolt holding him up was withdrawn. As he dropped several young men in the crowd fainted.

He struggled briefly and his body remained suspended for some forty-five minutes before being removed to the Hospital where it was prepared for burial in a prison grave.

1847 Thomas Leith

When Thomas Leith appeared at the High Court of Justiciary in Edinburgh on 1 September 1847 the charge was

That the prisoner, who resided in Hawkhill, Dundee, did, on or about 15th April last, wickedly and feloniously, and with intent to murder or grievously to injure the deceased Ann Welsh, his wife, mix, or procure to be mixed, with some barleymeal, which the prisoner expected to be used as food, a quantity of arsenic, or other deadly poison; and that his wife, on 21st April, caused the meal to be made into porridge, and that she soon thereafter became seriously ill and did, after lingering for several hours in a state of great suffering, die in consequence of having partaken of the porridge; and further, that the prisoner had previously evinced ill will and malice against his wife.

A newspaper report of the trial says that

the prisoner pleaded 'Not Guilty', in a feeble tone of voice.

The principal witness for the Crown was the Rev James Johnstone, who had been pastor of one of the local churches for eleven years. He confirmed that the couple had been regular churchgoers up until a few weeks prior to the murder when he had noticed that the accused had stopped attending.

Mrs Leith had spoken to him at one point saying that her husband

was very cruel to her in his address and manner, and that he had threatened to strike her.

Intriguingly, the witness also stated that he knew that a girl, Isabella Kenny, had lived in the accused's shop, where he sold clothes and small wares, from the winter of 1845 until she left in March or April 1846. He admitted he didn't know why she left.

The accused had also spoken to Mr Johnstone, telling him that he and his wife

could not live happily together, because they were not constituted alike.

Curiously, there had been an earlier incident where Thomas Leith apparently took ill after drinking tea made for him by his wife. That day, the witness had gone to the shop, which was just a couple-of-hundred yards from the house, where he spoke with the accused.

Leith had asked him if he had heard of the strange circumstance to which he had replied, 'It was a strange one indeed'. The witness had wanted the case examined but Leith, who had denied putting the poison into the tea himself, hadn't wanted the matter pursued. During the ensuing conversation with the witness he hadn't accused his wife outright but appeared to infer that she was the culprit.

Following that conversation Mr Johnstone had gone to speak with Mrs Leith and asked her directly if she knew anything about the poison. She denied knowing about it, saying she had made the tea and then taken her own before filling up the pot again and sending the rest down to her husband.

At least two of the witnesses at the trial swore that they had seen white particles floating in the tea, although any powder could only have been introduced by Mrs Leith or by Leith himself as a cover.

About three or four days later Leith again spoke to the pastor about separation, particularly in view of the poison incident. He said he wouldn't go home and his wife wouldn't cook anything for him anyway. On Wednesday 21 April Mr Johnstone had gone to the Leith's house where he found Mrs Leith lying on the kitchen bed with her knees drawn up to her stomach. Asked what was wrong she had replied that she had been sick since breakfast time.

The pastor had then gone to the shop where he had said the family were being poisoned and more or less ordered Leith to go and see them before fetching a doctor.

The accused had replied that they had tried to poison him and as that had failed they had done it to themselves. He then refused to leave the shop, prompting the witness to say that he must.

They went to the house and Leith left, apparently to fetch a doctor. Finding himself on his own with Mrs Leith, the pastor asked her what had happened. She explained that she had only a small amount of oatmeal in the house which she had used to make porridge for the children. There wasn't really enough to go round and she had taken a bag of barleymeal from the cupboard to make some more porridge. The barleymeal had been in the cupboard for about a month as she believed it had sand mixed in with it.

Only a small amount of the barleymeal porridge had been given to the children and she had eaten most of it. That was why the children, although ill, weren't as sick as she was. In saying all this, she made no mention of the accused or said whom she suspected.

Mr Johnstone went back to the shop where he found the accused. He asked Leith why he hadn't got a doctor and was told he had tried three without success.

The witness then went back to the house where he found Mrs Leith and the children, obviously very unwell.

A neighbour, Mrs Roy, met the accused at the door of the property and asked him outright if he had done this. Leith had made no reply but was described as being very agitated.

Despite that, the accused then put his hand on the witness's shoulder and said,

> I cannot tell you how much I will be obliged to you if you will go for a doctor.

The witness told the court he went for Dr Crichton who came and examined the patients.

The witness showed the doctor the bag of barleymeal and was asked by the medic to keep hold of it. Despite having been told not to throw out the remains of the porridge Mrs Roy had done so, although they were able to salvage a small amount, about enough to fill a small wine glass.

In addition, Dr Crichton twice used a stomach pump on Mrs Leith and the contents were also retained. The unfortunate woman died shortly afterwards.

According to the newspaper report, several other witnesses then corroborated Rev Johnston's evidence as to the death and to the widely held suspicion that the poison had been added to the porridge by the accused.

Dr Crichton confirmed and read from the report of the post-mortem carried out by himself and Dr Nimmo. Both were of the opinion that the deceased had died as a result of arsenic poisoning, the poison having been added to the porridge.

Another medic, Dr Douglas Maclagan, who had analysed the contents of the jar, bottles and bag, confirmed to the court that arsenic had been present in considerable quantity and certainly sufficient to cause death.

Evidence was led that Leith had ill-used his wife and kept her short of money. He was also said to have threatened to 'wash his hands in her heart's blood'.

Leith's character was further blackened by the fact that the young shop-girl, Isabella Kenny, gave evidence that he was the father of her child and she said he visited her and that she sent him letters, all of which caused friction between him and his wife.

With the prosecution also able to show that Leith had purchased arsenic – he had bought it, as most poisoners did, 'for pest control' – there was little hope for the accused.

Following the closing speeches and summing-up the jury took one-and-a-half hours to find the accused Guilty, by a majority. The Chancellor (foreman) of the jury also told the Judge that they unanimously recommended clemency.

Asked about their reasons the Chancellor said that several disapproved of the death penalty and that several would have brought in a verdict of Not Proven if they believed the prisoner would hang.

Lord Cochrane, who was obviously in no doubt as to the prisoner's guilt, said he would transmit their recommendation to the appropriate authorities, but said the law was quite clear and that he had no option but to sentence Leith to be hanged. Sentence was to be carried out in Dundee on 22 September.

The accused, who was described as being about thirty years of age and of respectable appearance, apparently accepted his sentence with great composure.

In fact the execution was delayed because of a number of applications to the Home Secretary for clemency for Leith.

One of those was launched by his sister who lobbied in Edinburgh before going to London where she had an audience with the Home Secretary. Sadly for her and her brother, the Home Secretary

> saw no grounds for recommending Her Majesty [Victoria] to exercise her prerogative in his behalf.

With the execution then set for Tuesday 5 October, his sister, who had tried so hard to save him from the scaffold was, along with other members of the family, among the last of his visitors. The family stayed for some time and Leith apparently repeated several times to his children that he had played no part in 'the death of their mother'.

Although Leith had harboured hopes that he might be reprieved, the newspaper reports suggested that even after these had been dashed he coped reasonably well, sleeping 'tolerably well' and entering into conversation with considerable animation with the different clergymen and other individuals who visited him.

Overnight, the workmen completed the building of the scaffold in front of the jail and members of the public came and went, all eager for a sight of the grisly apparatus. On the day of the execution a large number turned up to witness his fate.

Unsurprisingly, Leith had slept little that night and he was up and dressed by 4:00 am. A couple of hours later the usual group of reverend gentlemen arrived for the customary religious formalities.

By 7:00 am a considerable crowd had gathered and soon the area from the scaffold to the Overgate was a mass of individuals, reckoned to be between nine and ten thousand strong. Just a few minutes after 8:00 am Leith appeared along with the usual party of local dignitaries.

Leith himself, dressed 'in a handsome suit of black with white necktie', appeared calm. After exchanging a few words with Mr Renton, the Methodist minister, he announced:

> I leave the world to attend in a very few minutes at the bar of the God of truth, but I declare that I have had no more hand in the crime for which I was charged, and for which I am about to suffer the loss of my life, than any of those whom I now address. The unhappy differences which existed between me and my wife have doubtless been the cause of the crime being imputed to me, but, had the truth been told by the witnesses upon me instead of untruth, I would not have been in the unhappy position I now occupy. I leave my cause in my hands of that God before whose tribunal I am shortly to appear. I forgive all those who have spoken evil against me, and hope that they will be forgiven by God; and I trust he will forgive me.

Asked by the Rev Renton if he was guilty or not guilty Leith placed his hand on his heart and replied in a firm voice; 'I am Not Guilty'.

As the executioner adjusted the rope and placed the white hood over his head Leith repeated several times; 'O! Jesus, Jesus, save me by thy blood'. As he repeated this the drop fell and he struggled for some time before expiring.

He had asked for a cast of his head to be taken and this was done before his body was finally interred.

Aged about forty, Thomas Leith stood about five-feet-six-inches in height. Born into a poor family, he had married Ann Welsh when he was about twenty years old. The newspaper report suggests that they were soon estranged, although they had twelve children, of whom only six survived.

Through hard work and abstinence Leith had accumulated a bit of money and was the owner of a number of properties. At his death, he was reckoned to be worth around one thousand pounds which made him a man of some substance for his time.

He had been a follower of Methodism although, according to the newspapers, he had recently flirted with socialism. There were also suggestions that he was not particularly intelligent and he had become interested in phrenology, the study of the skull, and that was why he had the cast of his own made, so that it could be examined after his death.

The day before his execution he sent a letter to his children, commending religious virtue to them, telling them that God was just but that mankind had not been kind in its dealings with him.

Of course, some murderers continued to give voice to their innocence right up until the end but equally, many believers, on the basis that they were about to meet their Maker, would confess to their wrongdoings.

So was Leith in fact innocent? It appears from the evidence that the poison was in the bag on the shelf so Leith might not have intended it to be used by his wife. Alternatively, it may have been that he was aware she would use it at some point and had placed it there so that he wouldn't appear directly responsible.

That said, who else would have wanted Mrs Leith dead? Either it was a dreadful accident or he intended to be rid of his wife, perhaps so that he could live with Isabella Kenny.

Some sections of the media shared Lord Cochrane's view of the accused. A piece in the unfortunately named *Reformer's Gazette* described Leith as a monster who had murdered his wife and attempted to do the same to his own children. The paper's real vitriol however was reserved for the jury who had recommended mercy because some members disapproved of capital punishment, a view that had made a number flirt with a verdict of Not Proven.

The *Gazette* had strong views on the subject:

> We loathe such sentimentality. It is repugnant to law. It is repugnant to reason. They had simply to pronounce upon the facts on their oath to Almighty God; and there was nothing in this case to make the Jury swerve from their duty, painful as it was, far less to incur the guilt of perjury on their heads for such a man. If Burke and Hare [the infamous grave robbers turned murderers] had still to be tried, we do believe there are some sentimentalists among us who would have got up a petition for a reprieve to them.

The story of James Robertson is a particularly sad one even for a book on this topic.

Robertson was a farm servant or, in other words, a ploughman. A single man, he lived in the bothy, a rough-and-ready existence and no mistake, on the farm at Findowrie near Brechin. He was already the father of a five-year-old child and now he had fathered another child with Jean Duguid, a single lass who lived with her brother, Charles, at Inglismadie. The child had been born at Inglismadie on Friday 3 December 1847. On the Sunday, Robertson visited mother and child and asked her what she intended to do. She, not unreasonably, turned the question around and asked him what he was to do.

He told Jean that he would take the child and give it to his sister who lived at Turin, although Jean wasn't even sure that he had a sister living there. They were to meet the following Sunday, on the road between Inglismadie and Brechin, at a place close to Mains of Keithock. She agreed, always providing she was able.

In the event, poor Jean wasn't up to making the journey so another of Jean's brothers, Alexander, wrote to Robertson asking him to come to Inglismadie to collect the child.

Sometime between 8:00 and 9:00 pm the following Tuesday Robertson arrived to pick up the baby. Because it was so late and cold, Jean refused to part with the baby and Robertson said she would have to go to Findowrie with it.

Robertson later wrote a letter to Charles, asking Jean to bring the child and meet him at the Gallowhill in Brechin.

At around 1:00 pm on Christmas Eve 1847, accompanied by Mary Millar, Jean set off with the baby and met Robertson at the prearranged rendezvous about five hours later.

Jean asked if he had anyone to take the child to which Robertson replied that he didn't but he was going to take it to his sister, Jean Norie, at Unthank, who would look after it that night.

After that, he intended to take it to Alexander Young of Careston's wife who was to nurse the child. Everyone went to the Nories' house where Jean fed the child for the last time before his Jean Norie put it down in a cradle, after which, around 7:00 pm, Duguid and Mary left.

Robertson came out after her and told her she could visit the child at Careston but suggested she send word of her intention first.

About eight weeks later, Jean decided to visit the child and, presumably unannounced, went to Careston. Although there was an Alexander Young at Careston who was married, she wasn't able to see him or the baby.

Perhaps she was already suspicious as she got Alexander to write again to Robertson, this time asking where the baby was.

The child's father replied but Jean had to consult a solicitor in Brechin who wrote to Robertson, asking him to 'force a sight of the child', before matters finally moved forward.

Robertson replied directly to Jean, suggesting meeting at the Prentice Nook in Brechin the following Sunday. Jean and Charles met him and he told her, outwith her brother's hearing, that the child was dead.

She wanted to know when it had happened and he told her he 'had put away with it' and put it in a field. He didn't tell her where and she didn't ask.

Devastated by what she had been told Jean went to see Robertson's sister Jean at Unthank. Jean Norie asked after the child but, despite the fact that Robertson had told Jean Duguid not to say anything, she eventually poured out the sad tale.

Charles Duguid later told the court that he had accompanied his sister to the meeting with Robertson at the Prentice Nook but admitted he hadn't been a party to the conversation. He said his sister had told him afterwards that Robertson had 'put away with the child' and he had reported this to a police officer named Jack.

Robertson appeared at the Circuit Court on Saturday 22 April 1848, charged with

> having, on 24th December 1847, in the house occupied by William Norie, a servant on the farm of Unthank, near Brechin, got possession of a female illegitimate child, of which he was the father, and of having, on the adjoining farms of Cookston, Maisondieu, or Findowrie, suffocated it, by wrapping the clothes which were upon the child's person over its head, and in that way murdered it.

Robertson pleaded Not Guilty.

The accused's sister, Jean Norie, gave evidence that she had offered to keep the child herself but said the accused was concerned that his mother would realise the child's background and 'greet her hinderend'. He told her that a woman from Brechin would take the child.

Jean also told the court that she had been concerned when her brother took the baby away. Its face had almost been covered by the shawl and there was nothing to keep it off the baby's face. She was worried that it might slip over its face and her anxiety had kept her awake for most of the night.

The next time she had seen her brother was on the night of Auld Yule but her mother had been present all of the time which prevented her mentioning the child. (Auld Yule is an old Scottish tradition, now largely forgotten, where Christmas was celebrated under the old Julian calendar rather than the Gregorian one. This meant that Christmas was celebrated on 5 January and New Year on 12 January.)

William Jack, an officer of Forfarshire Rural Police gave evidence that he had been made aware of the statement on the evening of Sunday 5 March and he had gone to Findowrie at around 2:00 am the following morning where he arrested the accused. He had cautioned Robertson who nevertheless insisted on making a statement.

Robertson said,

> Well, I did make away with it, and buried it in the field east from the house there.

He continued he had

> done it on the night when I got it from its mother.

He then offered to show Constable Jack where it was buried. The witness suggested it was too dark but the accused insisted and showed him a spot near the steading where he said he had buried the body. Jack marked the spot with a stick.

The accused told Jack, he had 'smored [suffocated] it in its clothes'.

Jack later returned to the scene with Dr Mackie and found the body buried exactly where Robertson had said it was. The body was removed to Brechin in the care of Dr Mackie.

The next witness was Mrs Young, wife of Alexander Young, who stated that no one else of that name lived at Careston. She confirmed that she didn't know the accused and that she had never been asked by him to take charge of a child.

Dr Mackie of Brechin confirmed Jack's evidence about finding the body and said that it had been buried in a drain. It was fully dressed, probably about three or four weeks old. A report, written by himself and Dr Smith was read. Death appeared to have been caused by suffocation. He refuted a suggestion from the defence advocate that the child might have died of spasmodic croup.

Declarations dictated by the accused were read. Despite his plea, the accused

> fully admitted the whole circumstances, and stated that he had put away with the child because he was not able to support it. The child was smothered on his way home from Unthank to Findowrie, by wrapping its clothes tightly around its head. It was dead when he reached Findowrie, and he buried it in a drain with its clothes about it. He went home, not by the road, but across the fields.

The jury, having heard the closing speeches from both the advocate-depute for the Crown and the counsel for the prisoner and then heard Lord Moncrieff's summing up, took just minutes to unanimously find the accused Guilty, although they recommended mercy on account of the candour he had shown in admitting to the crime.

His Lordship said the recommendation would be sent to the proper quarter before pointing out that the last painful duty remained with him.

> He hoped in God that the recommendation of the jury might be favourably entertained; but he had to say the verdict was, in his opinion, in strict harmony with the evidence.

He then delivered a feeling address to the prisoner. The execution was fixed to take place 'in Forfar, on 10th May next, between the hours of eight and ten in the morning'.

It would appear that even their Lordships had some sympathy for the accused. Writing on Sunday 23 April 1848, one of their number, Lord Cockburn wrote in his diary:

> Getting on slowly, and dull, commonplace work. The audience was relieved yesterday by a murder. But it was a poor one. An infant suffocated in its clothes by its natural father. He was condemned, but won't be hanged.

The people of Brechin were of a similar view and they petitioned the Home Secretary seeking mercy but the response was short and to the point.

The Home Secretary had communicated with Lord Cockburn but regretted that he could find no grounds on which to recommend mercy and he did not feel he could do so

> without encouraging the expectation the deliberate murder of a child by its own father was not to be capitally punished.

A crowd, mostly females and children, thought to number around two thousand five hundred gathered on the east side of the prison gate in Forfar on 19 May to watch the execution of James Robertson.

10 *The old prison in Forfar*

Because the prison was then a little way north of the town itself the magistrates and town clerk left Forfar at around 7:00 am and gathered in the condemned cell where the executioner pinioned the prisoner. As ever, there were a number of ministers in attendance looking to spiritually prepare the condemned man for his execution.

At approximately 7:40 am the party assembled on the scaffold and the chaplain at the gaol, the Rev Harry Stuart of Oathlaw, offered up 'a short but impressive prayer'.

Robertson had insisted on being hooded in the prison as he didn't wish to look on the crowd, he took his place on the drop, gave the signal and the bolt was withdrawn. A fall of five feet saw him dead within just two minutes, apparently without a struggle.

He had left various writings, partly his own work and partly the Governor's but all dictated by him.

Robertson appeared to have found God but he also had a more practical message, suggesting

> the farmers and others employing the young and unthoughtful of both sexes, place a barrier between them, and prevent them coming together as much as possible, as this has been my ruin; and may the young and unthoughtful in me see that God will not allow the wicked to go unpunished. Oh! May the young men who are living in the bothies take warning, and be guarded against the wiles of wicked and lustful desires.

Perhaps the most poignant was a letter written to the Rev Stuart who had campaigned far and wide, including travelling to Edinburgh to speak with the judges in the case, in his attempts to have Robertson's sentence commuted to life imprisonment.

> Oh! That I had done as my pious parents wanted me. They wanted me to learn a trade, and to take more schooling, but I had no inclination to do anything but work horses. I was fee'd away when I was fourteen years of age. I lived always after that in a bothy, where I never saw any good, but much evil – The women-servants have been my ruin. Oh! Warn them not to come near the bothies, and so entice away young boys ... Oh! That had I my life to begin again, and to warn others to flee from temptation and sinful ways, and not be put off and depend on a death-bed repentance, for I fear they be too late!

Robertson's grave was marked by a simple stone built into the north wall of the prison. It reads 'J R 19 May 1848'.

11 *This stone marks the spot where James Robertson was buried*

Child murder was commonplace in the nineteenth century and another was recorded in 1862, although in this tragic case the perpetrator was the mother.

Rumours had been circulating in parts of Montrose for some time that Margaret Stewart, a single woman aged about twenty-two, had given birth, although no one had seen the child. Margaret, who it was reported had been employed as a servant by a respectable family until just before the rumours had started, was eventually arrested and charged with
> having made away with a child to which she had given birth about the beginning of March.

The situation had come to the notice of the local police on Friday 14 March when an acquaintance, who had heard that Margaret had been arrested, sent another person to the Police Office to ask if this was true. In fact the police had no knowledge of the rumours but, suspicions aroused by the odd nature of the inquiry, the officer on duty, a Mr Brownlee, asked for the girl's details and decided to investigate further. Aware that the girl lived with her father in the North Links, Mr Brownlee, accompanied by Sergeant Mollison, made his way there but, unwilling to cause any unnecessary alarm, decided to speak to a neighbour, Mrs Rankine, first to see if she could confirm the truth or otherwise of the allegations.

Whatever Mrs Rankine had to say must have concentrated the policemen's thoughts as they quickly sought and obtained a warrant for the arrest of Margaret Stewart, who was then arrested at a revival prayer meeting in Queen Street.

The allegations were put to the prisoner who initially protested her innocence but once in the police office admitted that she had given birth to a baby boy and hidden the body in the attic. A search of the house was carried out and, after about an hour, the body was discovered. The corpse was examined by Drs Johnston and Lawrence and a full post-mortem was carried out the following day.

There is no record of the outcome other than it is obvious that the findings were anything but favourable to the prisoner. As a result, the prisoner was transferred to Forfar where she was examined by Sheriff Guthrie Smith before being committed to the prison there.

The outcome of an examination of the case by the Procurator-Fiscal was sent to the Crown authorities and Stewart, charged with child murder, with an alternative charge of concealment of pregnancy, was indicted to stand trial at the Circuit Court in Perth the following month. As one might imagine, the incident was the cause of much speculation in the town, not least because of the girl's revivalist beliefs.

The Court started on Tuesday 15 April but such was the backlog of cases that it was the following Monday before Stewart's case was called. The formal charge was that

> on Tuesday 5th March, on or near the cottar house at Southfield, Links, Montrose, occupied by James Stewart, wayman, in the service of the Scottish North-Eastern Railway Company, she did give birth to a living male child, and did immediately or soon after its birth, attack and assault the said child, and did compress its neck and throat by means of a cord or other ligature, which she tied or drew tightly round its neck, and did thus strangle or suffocate it; and did strike it one or more severe blows on or near the head, or did in some other manner inflict injuries on or near the head of the said child, by which it was mortally injured, and from which it died and was thus murdered.

The trial judge, Lord Ardmillan, put it to the accused that she had been charged with child murder and also the crime of concealment of pregnancy and asked whether she was pleading guilty or not guilty?

Her counsel, Mr Nevay, advised that his client pled Guilty to concealment of pregnancy and the Advocate-Depute intimated that he would accept her plea. (There are several other instances of mothers having a similar plea accepted.)

On her behalf, Mr Nevay pointed out that his client had previously been of good character and that this was her first offence and suggested that, with the main charge against his client withdrawn, His Lordship might think it sufficient to sentence her to a short term of imprisonment.

Lord Ardmillan agreed that with the child murder charge dropped the court could pronounce a much lighter sentence and, after making a number of remarks about her lifestyle, sent her to prison for twelve months.

I would suspect that Margaret Stewart considered herself lucky in the circumstances, although the biggest difference between her case and that of James Robertson was simply that, even in those days, it was probably understood that she had acted out of desperation while Robertson had obviously cold-bloodedly planned to murder his child.

Perhaps too, there was some understanding and sympathy in that the poor girl had been abandoned by the child's father, whether he was someone from her own class, or perhaps her former employer or a member of his family, a regular occurrence in those days.

1865 Andrew Brown

In the early afternoon of Wednesday 6 September 1865 the schooner *Nymph* was towed out from the harbour at Montrose into the waters of the North Sea where she set course for London.

The *Nymph* had a crew of four, consisting of the Captain, John Greig junior, who was also the son of the ship's owner, the mate Andrew Brown, and two crewmen, John Pert and Alexander Raeburnes.

It was a warm day and, after a few remarks about the weather, Greig lay down on the deck for a snooze.

As they sailed past Red Head, more or less opposite the village of Inverkeillor, Pert, who was at the tiller, heard two heavy thumps. He turned to see Greig lying with his head, literally, split in two and Brown raising an axe to deliver another blow.

Brown managed to get in a third blow before Pert rushed at him, and, after a brief wrestling match, grabbed the axe and threw it overboard. The Mate seemed to understand what he had done as, after about ten minutes, he remarked, 'I have done the deed, and I will suffer for it'.

One can imagine the situation on the vessel. Raeburnes was an old man and not physically able for confrontation so both he and Pert must have had serious concerns about their own safety.

The two crewmen suggested returning to Montrose but when Brown insisted on sailing to Stonehaven, to see his mother he said, there was, understandably, no objection from them.

At one point Brown asked the pair, individually, if they would help him throw the body over the side but both refused. Then Raeburnes climbed onto the rigging to wave to another Montrose vessel but was told to come down by Brown, otherwise, he threatened, 'I'll heave you over the side'.

Brown's only explanation for the attack was that it was to do with an old grudge. No one dared to question him further.

At one point Brown told Pert,

Jack, it's a good job you got the axe, or else you would have got the same.

Later, as they passed Montrose on the journey north, Brown commented, 'I've got another man to kill'. Sometime after, he asked Pert for the loan of a knife. Pert, unsurprisingly, replied 'No', although he said later that he didn't consider the one remark was connected with the other.

During the journey, each member of the crew took a turn at steering, although Brown actually took the tiller for three or four hours without a break. Giving evidence at the trial, Pert said that, during that time, Brown had 'cracked' away to him, almost as if nothing had happened. About an hour after the murder he asked Pert; 'Jack, will you come to see me hanged?' No doubt mindful of his own safety, Pert didn't reply. Later, Brown asked Pert for a shilling, saying he had sixpence and that would be the last one shilling and sixpence he would ever give his mother.

The murder had taken place at about 5:00 pm and it was around midnight when they arrived off Stonehaven but the seven-hour journey must have seemed much longer to the frightened crewmen.

A pilot boat came out from Stonehaven carrying, by a bizarre coincidence, two of Brown's uncles. When one of them came on board, Brown showed him the body before running forward and trying to drop the ship's anchor, presumably in a forlorn attempt to prevent the ship docking.

As they came alongside the pier, Raeburnes jumped ashore and Pert quickly followed, leaving Brown and the pilot on board.

The two crewmen made for the police office where they told their dreadful tale. In the meantime, Brown had gone to his mother's house where he was later arrested.

The trial began in Edinburgh on 8 January 1866. Brown pled Not Guilty and lodged a special defence that at the time of the murder he 'was labouring under insanity'.

After relating the sequence of events on board the *Nymph*, both Pert and Raeburnes told the court that they didn't believe that Brown had been under the influence of alcohol at the time of the attack.

Certainly, they accepted that he had had a drink or two but they didn't feel that he was drunk as such.

Even the dead man's father, John Greig senior, gave evidence that Brown 'was temperate for a sailor'.

In his evidence, Andrew Brown, uncle of the accused and one of the two pilots who had come out to the *Nymph* to guide her into Stonehaven, expressed his shock at finding what his nephew had done.

He had a different story to tell as regards Brown's condition.

> I knew by his voice when he spoke first that he was not sober. I can tell perfectly from his voice when he is the worse of drink.

Giving his evidence, Sergeant John Gartly said that when he arrested Brown the accused had replied, 'This is a bad job sergeant, but he was a bad fellow,' and then told him that Greig had led him to the bad houses of London where he spent his money so that he had nothing to take to his mother.

In fact there was no evidence to suggest that the Captain was of bad character or that he and his mate had anything other than a good relationship.

The sergeant also stated that he smelt drink on Brown and that he was under the influence when arrested.

For the defence, Elizabeth Brown, a sister of the accused, told the court that her brother had fallen into a ship's hold when he was eight or nine years old and he had complained of headaches for ever afterwards.

He had never been a strong boy and about four years before, she had noticed changes in his behaviour after he had been injured in another accident aboard another ship.

Two of the local doctors had performed a very painful operation on her brother and he had never been the same afterwards. The accidents and operation had changed his character altogether and when he was drunk he now became very violent. Then, about a year before the murder, he had been struck on the head by a falling block.

When he arrived at his mother's house on the day of the murder he had been very much the worse for drink and said, 'It was the drink that did it all'.

Other witnesses gave similar accounts of Brown's health and the effect drink seemed to have on him.

Following the addresses by the Crown and defence and the summing-up of the Judge, the jury retired to consider their verdict. They took just over fifty minutes to find the accused Guilty, although a minority recommended mercy.

There could only be one sentence but there were practical difficulties in establishing where the execution should take place.

Brown was kept in the prison in Forfar, where he would receive only bread and water, until 31 January when he would be taken to Montrose where the sentence was to be carried out.

Although other alternatives were considered, it was thought that, as the murder had taken place at sea some eight miles south of Montrose, on board a Montrose ship and the victim had been local, the town should be where Brown met his end.

The townspeople were not unduly happy about the idea and petitioned to have the execution carried out elsewhere and *The Montrose, Arbroath and Brechin Review*, as it was then known, suggested that the local people

were anxious that the town should be relieved from the dread spectacle. Apparently, this high moral argument was not the main reason for looking to have the execution elsewhere. Quite simply, the 'host' burgh was required to meet the expense of the execution and the local folk resented meeting the not inconsiderable costs.

The whole episode was made more difficult by the fact that the local jail in Montrose was closed so the prisoner was required to stay in the prison at Forfar until the day of his execution.

Tom Valentine

12 *The old prison in Montrose*

13 *The Eagle Inn, George Street, Montrose. The hangman, William Calcraft, stayed there prior to executing Andrew Brown*

In 1866 the Montrose jail was situated in George Street, south of what is now the George Hotel, and the execution was to take place outside the building and the authorities intended to use the slope of the upper part of George Street as a sort of gallery for spectators. (The picture shows the old police station. The building just out of sight on the right of the old prison was the Eagle Inn. The site is now occupied by the George Hotel.)

Crush barriers were erected to help control the crowd and it was thought that a crowd of up to thirty-thousand people could be accommodated in the area. In the end, only around two thousand turned up but the *Review* believed

the authorities were wise to take the precautions they adopted.

As a further means of crowd control, one hundred and fifty of the merchants and other electors were recruited as special constables under the control of ex-Bailie Guthrie, who was appointed Captain for no other reason than that he had performed the same duty when Margaret Shuttleworth, the last woman to be hanged in Montrose, had been executed forty-four years earlier.

A gibbet, hired from Aberdeen, was erected just beside the old police station and prison in George Street.

With the top of the beam some eighteen feet in the air and the platform ten feet from the ground, the apparatus dominated the site and proved to be the subject of much morbid curiosity as most of those present had never seen such a thing before.

The *Review* reported that the crowd was largely composed 'of strangers and the lower orders of society' and 'a large representation of sailors and fishermen and also not a few females'. Many of those present excused themselves by declaring they had come only to see the scaffold or Calcraft, the hangman.

Wisely, the authorities had arranged with the managers at the various factories to keep their workers engaged until just after 2:00 pm when Calcraft's work would be completed, in order to keep the attendance at a minimum.

On the day of the execution, Brown was brought from Forfar on an early train, reaching Montrose just after 5:00 am, although even then, there were already a few spectators as well as the official party to see him arrive.

After the formalities, Calcraft performed his unpleasant duty before the body was removed to the prison where two doctors pronounced life to be extinct.

The body was taken by hearse to the station and then by train to Forfar where Brown's remains were buried in a corner of the prison garden.

So ended the incident described as the Red Head murder. Thankfully, that was the last ever public execution in the area – the practice of public executions was brought to an end by the Capital Punishment Amendment Act 1868.

1872   Thomas Scobbie

Gamekeeper George Spalding lived with his father Robert, sister Jane and her son, also George, and another sister, Susan, in a cottage just north of the old Dundee–Arbroath turnpike road.

On the morning of Tuesday 24 September Jane had washed and hung out two of George's flannel shirts on a rope in nearby Kingennie Wood. It was only later, when she went to hang out more washing, that she noticed they had disappeared, presumably stolen.

She went back to the house and told her brother who happened to be at home at the time. He went off to see if he could find anyone who might have taken the items. Young George was out tending to the animals but later the two met up and went off together.

Later, young George returned, saying that his uncle had found a man, which his mother took to mean the man who had taken the shirts. She then left the cottage and found her brother and the man, whom she later discovered was Thomas Scobbie, who said he knew where the shirts were.

She offered to go with them but her brother sent her away and a little while later they returned with Scobbie carrying the shirts. Her brother then announced that he would take Scobbie to Monifieth police office, about forty-five minutes walk away.

The two men, accompanied by the gamekeeper's brown retriever bitch, Juno, set off at around 4:00 pm. At around 10:00 pm Juno returned on her own and, although Jane was concerned for her brother's safety, she knew that on occasion his duties kept him out all night so it was possible that something work-related had detained him

Early the following morning there was still no sign of George senior so Jane and her son, accompanied by Juno, set off to look for the missing man.

It was obvious that the dog was troubled in some way and, when they reached the junction of the Arbroath road and the Kirk road leading to Monifieth the dog stopped and refused to go beyond a clump of bushes beside a ditch.

Jane moved the bushes aside to find the body of her brother half-hidden in the undergrowth. Had it not been for the dog the body might have lain undetected for some time.

It seemed reasonable to assume that the man George was escorting to the police station had committed the murder, although there were initially suggestions of the possible involvement of a second man who had been seen, apparently following the pair.

The thief, a tramp called Thomas Scobbie, was soon traced and arrested on the night of Thursday 26 September. Scobbie was taken to Spalding's cottage in the early hours of Friday morning where Jane Spalding identified him as the man she had seen with her brother.

By the weekend the police knew much about Scobbie's personal history. He had been in the army and had married in Aberdeen. His estranged wife lived in Cotton Road in Dundee and he had recently been employed at Seafield Works but had walked out the previous Monday without giving any explanation.

The police were also able to announce that they had traced the second man and that he would be witness in the forthcoming trial.

After Scobbie's arrest the police had searched his room at the model lodging-house where he lived and found pawn tickets, dated the day of the murder, hidden in the leaves of a Bible. Subsequently, they were able to recover shirts and other items of clothing from the pawnbrokers. Evidence gathering appears to have been becoming more focused and when the clothes were examined, grasses and leaves, similar to those to be found at the murder scene, were discovered sticking to the coat and trousers. The coat and trousers also had cuts and tears on them, thought to have been the work of Spalding's dog. A number of bloodstained shirts were also recovered.

Scobbie appeared at the Circuit Court in Dundee on Tuesday 8 April 1873 where he tendered a plea of Not Guilty.

Jane Spalding gave evidence about the events on the day of the murder and confirmed that the accused was the man brought back to the cottage by her brother. He had said that the shirts had been taken by his neighbour, although he didn't explain who his neighbour was or how he came to know where the shirts were.

She also confirmed that the bonnet he had on that day was like the one produced in court, except that then it had had two ribbons on it. The witness also confirmed that when the police brought him to the cottage on the Friday he had been wearing a different set of clothes.

Giving his evidence, eleven-year-old George Spalding said he had returned from herding between 2:00 and 3:00 pm on the day of the murder and it was then his grandfather, Robert, had told him about the missing shirts.

He confirmed that he had met his uncle and that they saw a man in a nearby field. His uncle had gone up to the man and said, 'Deliver up the shirts'.

The man had replied that he didn't have them but knew where they were. He said his neighbour had taken them. The three walked down part of the old turnpike road and soon came across the shirts lying in a hole underneath the hedge.

As they walked back to the cottage, his uncle had said he would take the accused to Monifieth. The man hadn't said anything at that time. After finding his uncle's body the following day he and his mother had walked to Ethiebeaton Farm where they spoke to farm workers Robert Alexander and George Nicoll who harnessed a horse and cart.

The witness then went with Alexander to Monifieth to report the murder and when they returned the body was removed in the cart.

Just then, young George noticed the missing shirts lying just yards from the body and he also saw a man 'hanging about'. He was certain it was the accused.

George Nicoll told the court that when he saw the body it had been 'happed up' (covered over) and the bramble bush also helped hide the body. There were marks further down the road, as if there had been a struggle, although he couldn't say whether or not the body had been dragged to the spot where it was found.

Various other witnesses testified to seeing the accused, both on his own and with George Spalding, in the area on the day of the murder. Other witnesses, Melville Suttie and David Mollison, slaters from Dundee, had been making their way home after working at one of the local farms, and had seen the deceased and the accused wrestling with each other. Mollison testified that he heard the accused threaten the deceased that he would 'do for him'. The witnesses thought about watching the proceedings but, deciding there was no danger, elected to go home.

Alexander Hutcheson, an iron-turner from Monifieth, told the court he had found a piece of ribbon, which he identified as one of the productions in court, about ten yards away from where the body had been found and that he had noticed that the grass there 'was much trampled'. He had taken the ribbon and given it to Mrs Marnoch at the police station.

Constable Marnoch told the court of his first sight of the body and how he gone to the Spalding's cottage at around midday where he had searched the pockets of the deceased.

Edward Rowan, a pawnbroker in Dundee, confirmed that the accused was the man who had pawned various items of clothing between six and seven o'clock on the night of the murder. He had given the man, who had said his name was John Young, nine shillings (45p) for the items.

The items were taken away by the police on 1 October and it was only when he was handing them over that he noticed that the trousers and coat were torn and that there were 'burrs and seeds attached to them'. Margaret Millan or Bryan, an assistant at a neighbouring pawnbrokers, told the court that the accused had pawned four shirts in the name of James Smith just before seven o'clock on the same night.

The accused sometimes lodged with Elizabeth Littlejohn and Peter Kelly, a couple who lived together as husband and wife, and he had gone into their house at around half-past-eight on the Tuesday night. His face was scratched and Littlejohn told the court she had given him a piece of cloth and he had wiped the blood from his face.

When he came in she saw that he was wearing a long topcoat and she also noticed his bonnet had only one ribbon. It had always had two ribbons on it before that day.

The witness also swore that Scobbie couldn't have spent the afternoon in the house as it was locked up. The key was still where she had left it when she returned home at 6:00 pm so she knew that Kelly had been out all afternoon.

Scobbie also stayed on occasion at the model lodging-house referred to earlier and the keeper, James Oudney, gave evidence that the prisoner had a chest in his room there. The accused hadn't slept there on the night of the twenty-fourth but had returned the following night, although he didn't sleep there that night either. He had returned again on the Thursday and was arrested later that day.

The witness told the police about the chest and he was present when they searched it and found the two pawn tickets.

Another witness, William Fraser, a turnkey employed by Dundee police, told the court he had searched the accused after his arrest and found a clasp-knife. He also confirmed that the prisoner was wearing a bonnet with only one ribbon.

Inspector Adams of Forfarshire Constabulary told the court that when he first saw Scobbie he noticed scratches on his face. They were quite large, certainly larger than might have been made by contact with bushes and he felt it more likely that they had been made by someone's fingernails.

When the witness asked Scobbie how he had come by the scratches he had answered that a Mrs Ross had hit him in the face with an umbrella. The allegation that she had scratched the accused's face with an

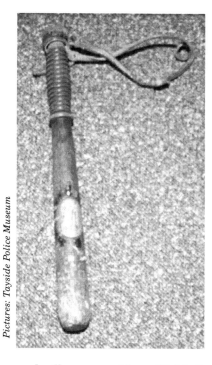

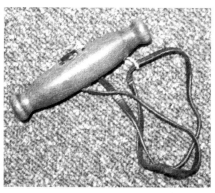

15 *Before handcuffs were developed, leather thongs such as these were in regular use and were still being used in the 1950s*

14 *A baton of the type used by Forfarshire police during Victorian times*

umbrella, or seen him with his face scratched, was later denied by Mrs Isabella Miller or Ross.

The Inspector also testified that he had visited the crime scene where he had noted small seeds and burrs, similar to those found on the jacket of the prisoner.

Medical evidence was given by Dr Campbell of Dundee who, accompanied by Dr Ritchie, had carried out the post-mortem on the deceased. He reported that the head-wounds, which appeared to have been inflicted with the handle of the clasp-knife, would have been sufficient to induce stupor. Once the victim was in that state, strangulation would have been much easier and he believed that the deceased was strangled by an assailant's right hand pressing on the front of the throat.

Certainly the post-mortem showed that the deceased had been generally healthy and there was no possibility that he had died from natural causes. Similarly, the witness said that the injuries to the body were certainly not accidental and couldn't have been self-inflicted.

Dr Campbell also testified that he had examined the accused's shirt and found three red marks which he took to be blood. This had been distributed as follows:

one minute spot on the right wristband, and two on the upper edge and front of the neckband – the one about half an inch to the right, and the other one inch to the left, of the middle panel of the said band, corresponding in situation to the wounds found on neck of William Thoms or Scobbie [other names used by the accused].

Some particles were removed by us from one of the stains on neckband above mentioned, and subjected to a careful microscopic examination, when we found amidst fibres of cloth numerous blood corpuscles, some isolated and quite circular, others in groups and less perfect in outline.

The prisoner's declaration was then read out:

My name is Thomas Scobbie I am aged thirty-six years, and I am a labourer, am married, and reside in the Model Lodging house in Overgate, Dundee. I am not guilty of the charge of murder made against me. Being interrogated – Where were you on Tuesday last, 24th current, and more particularly where were you in the afternoon and evening of that day? I declare I was in the town of Dundee the whole of that day. I was back and forward all afternoon, between my own lodging-house and the house of a fiddler named Kelly, a lame man, who lives in the Overgate. I sat in his house for the greater part of the afternoon. I have nothing more to say. All of which I declare to be the truth. Signed 'Thomas Scobbie'

This closed the Crown case and, with no evidence led by the defence, the Advocate-Depute then addressed the jury and asked for a verdict of guilty.

Mr Scott for the prisoner contended that; there was no evidence as to what happened between the point when the men were last seen and the time the body was discovered; but even on the supposition that Scobbie had killed Spalding, there was no room to lead to any other verdict than that of culpable homicide (manslaughter).

The judge then addressed the jury. A contemporary press report says; 'Lord Deas charged strongly against the prisoner', which would suggest a fairly biased summing up.

The proceedings had shown the flimsy alibi put forward by Scobbie to be false and the evidence against him, although largely circumstantial because of the limited scientific knowledge of the period, was nevertheless damning.

Today, of course, samples would have been taken from the deceased's fingernails, bloods matched and samples of the greenery at the crime scene taken and compared with that found on the pawned clothes.

Nevertheless, the fifteen-man jury had little doubt about the identity of the perpetrator of the crime and took just ten minutes to come to a unanimous verdict of Guilty, although a majority (14–1) did recommend leniency.

In passing sentence Lord Deas pointed out that the question of leniency was a matter for Her Majesty (Victoria) and the recommendation would be passed to the appropriate officials.

He then donned the black cap and read the formal sentence:

> In respect of the said verdict of assize against the panel, Lord Deas and Lord Jerviswoode decern and adjudge the said Thomas Scobbie, panel to be carried from the bar back to the prison of Dundee, therein to be detained, and fed on bread and water only, until Tuesday, the twenty-ninth of April next to come, and upon that day, betwixt the hours of eight and ten o'clock, forenoon, within the walls of the said prison to be hanged by the neck upon the gibbet, by the hands of the common executioner, until he be dead, and ordain his body thereafter to be buried within the walls of the said prison, which is pronounced for doom.

As was customary, he added the words,

> And may God have mercy on your soul.

Just two weeks later, Scobbie's lawyer announced that he had received a letter from the Home Secretary acknowledging receipt of a letter, signed by several jurymen, stating they hadn't understood that they could have returned a verdict of culpable homicide.

The official document from the Secretary of State, announcing the respite of the sentence of death passed on Scobbie, was received by Provost Cox of Dundee on Saturday 26 April.

The hangman, William Calcraft, who was already in the city, expressed his gratification that his services were not to be required as, he said,

> though executioner, he felt almost as much grieved in carrying out the sentence of death as the unhappy man who was to suffer it.

The same newspaper report said the hangman

> left for London on Saturday evening. His assistant had been engaged for Ayr, as Calcraft had refused to go there.

(The reference to Ayr is confusing as the last recorded execution there was in 1854.)

In truth, the debate about culpable homicide got their Lordships off a legal hook of their own making. There was presumption that once someone had been sentenced to death the execution should be carried out within a reasonable time. What Lord Deas had forgotten was that the month of April had started so that when he announced that the execution would take place on Tuesday 29 April *yet to come*, he was effectively postponing the sentence until 1880. Apart from that, he had sentenced the prisoner to be fed only bread and water until then. In the circumstances, the authorities were probably delighted to have a get-out so Scobbie's sentence was commuted to a period of imprisonment and he was finally released in 1897. He is believed to have died shortly after.

This case had at least one novel approach to solving the crime and, according to folklore at least, an even more bizarre attempt to obtain a confession.

During the initial investigation, Spalding's dog, Juno, was taken into the cell where Scobbie was being held. Faced with the man alleged to have murdered her master the dog remained unperturbed and showed no sign of recognition.

The other tale, widely repeated but apparently without foundation, is that, in keeping with an old superstition referred to by James VI of Scotland in his book *Daemonologie*, the guilt of the accused was tested in the oddest way.

This superstition, known as trial or ordeal by bier, widely known throughout Europe in medieval times, was that if a murder touched his victim then the corpse would begin to bleed. Sometimes it was thought that if the perpetrator even approached the body of his victim that would be sufficient.

In Scotland, it had been used in the trial of Philip Standsfield in 1688. Standsfield was accused of strangling his father and throwing the body into a river. After a simple post-mortem had been carried out Standsfield was asked to lift the body up and, when he did so, blood came from one of the cuts.

Despite his advocate putting forward a strong defence that this 'evidence' was no more than superstition which could give no indication of guilt or innocence Standsfield was found guilty and executed.

In Scobbie's case, he was apparently taken into the presence of the body and asked if he had committed the dreadful act. Sadly for the investigators Scobbie swore that he was innocent and the corpse failed to bleed or show any sign that would have incriminated the accused.

Quite how seriously a court might have viewed such 'evidence' in the 1870s we can only surmise. If the tale is true however it is odd that it was attempted in a case where simple forensic evidence was used to convict the accused.

North Street in Montrose was the scene of another murder in October 1872. The perpetrator, James White, was a retired butcher, then aged fifty.

Sadly, White was obviously suffering from some form of mental illness and not responsible for his actions.

He was a man of some means as he owned property in both Brechin and Montrose and was believed to have been a member of the Metropolitan Police Force in London before he came to Montrose.

Reports of the murder suggest that he had been due to appear at the Circuit Court in Dundee in February 1872, although no indication is given of the nature of the action. (The writer could find no record of the circuit court in Dundee during that period.)

White apparently took the train to Dundee and answered his name on the first day but then disappeared. The authorities assumed that he had taken his own life and a search was made in the harbour at Dundee but no body was found.

Almost as mysteriously, White reappeared in Montrose almost a fortnight later. He refused to explain his absence, saying only that he had been staying with a friend in Glenesk.

He had previously carried on a butcher's business in Murray Street and had a good reputation but after his disappearance he gave up his shop, although he continued dealing in cattle for a time before he eventually gave that up too.

His problem would appear to have been what we would now call depression, although his condition was obviously much more serious than that. The newspaper report described him as having fallen into 'a dull and spiritless condition', adding that he rarely left his home.

Just six weeks previously, his own doctor, Dr Kay, had recommended to Mrs White that she have her husband put into an asylum. The unfortunate woman had refused, partly because of the expense but mainly because she had no concerns about him doing her or any of their five boys and one girl any harm. Indeed, there seemed to be no suggestion that White was in fact a danger to anyone except perhaps himself.

In fact, White was more seriously ill than anyone suspected. Either that or the medicine he was taking to help him sleep may have had serious side effects.

At about lunchtime on that fateful day the younger children had just gone out to play on the green in front of the house and the daughter, who was aged eighteen, had gone upstairs leaving the parents in the kitchen. The girl heard her father come upstairs before going back down again and, she assumed, leaving the house.

Moments later, the youngest child, a boy aged three, went back into the house before running out shouting to the others to come and see their mother. The daughter, hearing his cries, ran down to find her mother's body on the kitchen floor. She believed her mother was still alive and a neighbour called to the scene thought that she too could feel a pulse.

When Dr Robb, Dr Kay's assistant, arrived, he pronounced the poor woman dead, caused by her having been struck a single blow to the head. Word was immediately sent to Dr Kay who alerted the police.

Superintendent Wilson was at the murder-scene conducting his investigations when he was advised that Mrs White's mother, an elderly lady aged seventy-three, had been assaulted in the single room she occupied at the corner of Upper Hall Street and Market Street.

She too had been struck on the head and, although she lived for a number of hours, dying at the infirmary about nine o'clock that night, she was unable or unwilling to give any information about her assailant. Nevertheless, it was quickly established that she too had been attacked and murdered by White.

White was seen making his way along Market Street before passing down New Wynd and into Baltic Street. At one point he met a neighbour and remarked to him that he had

killed two devils and was on his way to kill another one.

Later, he was seen on the Suspension Bridge (**14**) by two local men, Robert Orkney, a mussel-dredger, and a mechanic called Davidson. In a conversation with them he asked if they could see devils and pointed to the water, asking if they could see them. The two men assumed he had been drinking and replied accordingly.

Suddenly, White grabbed hold of one of the rails and somersaulted over the side into the river. Two shore labourers, John Levan and James Ross, heard the cries that there was someone in the water and they launched a boat and rowed out into the river.

16 *The old Chain or Suspension Bridge at Montrose - scene of White's attempt to kill more devils!*

They reached White but could only keep him afloat as their boat was too small to try to lift him up into it. Charles Pert, one of the ferrymen, had launched a ship's boat and he arrived at the scene and was able to get the half-drowned man on board.

As they made their way back to the shore they attempted to resuscitate White and by the time they reached the beach he was conscious but incoherent. A nonswimmer, White was lucky, if that word could be used in the circumstances, to be alive, as the current had carried him down river on the surface of the water for some three- or four-hundred yards.

He told his rescuers,

> Seven devils have been chasing me. I have killed two of them, and will get the others yet.

White was found to have in his possession a small butcher's axe which appears to have been the murder weapon in both instances.

He was taken to the Infirmary where he was treated while under 'strict police surveillance'. The following day, the Procurator-Fiscal arrived to view the crime scenes. He also visited the Infirmary, although he made no contact with White himself.

Unsurprisingly, the local press reported:

> As the news spread throughout the town, the most painful excitement was created, and it is needless to say that the tragedy soon became the all absorbing topic of conversation among the inhabitants. A considerable

number of the inhabitants also visited the Suspension Bridge, and speculation was rife as to the exact spot from which the murderer had thrown himself into the water.

Once he was well enough, White was taken to Forfar where he was examined. The results were not made known officially although it was understood that White was not fit enough mentally to be judicially examined.

Initially, White was taken to the jail in Dundee before being removed to the 'lunatic ward' at Perth Prison. There he made an unsuccessful attempt to commit suicide before he eventually succeeded by throwing himself down a stairwell on 9 December.

The distance was less than eight feet but the fall was sufficient to bring White's troubled life to an end.

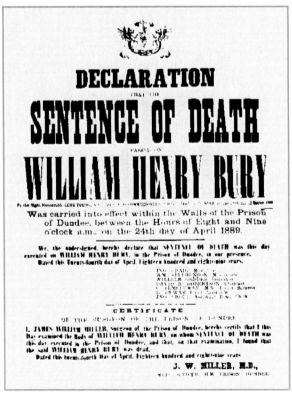

17 *Notice of the carrying out of the death sentence on William Bury*

One of the most fascinating murder tales from Tayside is that of William Bury for, although the killing itself was nothing out of the ordinary for the period, there was speculation that he might have been Jack the Ripper.

In truth, Bury was probably little more than a boastful and conceited, alcoholic conman with a track record as a liar and a cheat. Born in Wolverhampton, he had moved to London when he was just eighteen, no doubt believing, or at least hoping, that the streets were literally paved with gold.

He made a living of sorts as a sand and sawdust seller, touting those commodities round the local pubs in the Bromley-by-Bow area of the capital. Bury worked for a man named James Martin who effectively leased him a horse, cart and a stable for sixteen shillings (80p) per week. Martin also sold him the sawdust so that any profit made belonged to Bury. Presumably Bury got credit however because after he left Martin's employ he was still due him over £17.

The sawdust business was not Martin's only source of income however as he and his partner, Kate Spooner, also ran a brothel and Ellen Elliott was employed there, ostensibly as a domestic servant.

Medically, Ellen wasn't very strong which had resulted in her receiving very little schooling but in one material aspect she was certainly different from other women from the same background. Quite simply, Ellen had a bit of money. An aunt had died some years before and left Ellen a legacy of around £300 which she had prudently invested in shares in the Union Bank. This figure may not seem like a lot today but in the late 1880s the dividends would have provided useful income to a working-class girl like Ellen.

Ellen's windfall was widely known and there seems little doubt that Bury saw an opportunity to get his hands on the money. He proposed to Ellen and they were married on 2 April, Easter Monday, 1888.

From the start the marriage was in difficulties for not only was Bury an alcoholic but he was also allergic to hard work. One of the shares in the Bank was sold so that Bury could buy his own horse and cart but unfortunately the pony was unsound and had to be sold at a substantial loss. In addition, Bury's drink problem got worse and he did little or no work, preferring to rely on Ellen's money.

Within weeks of their marriage he was physically abusing Ellen and trying to force her into giving him money. Presumably she still had some regular income and Bury would simply take her money from her purse. At one point, the situation was so bad that she took some of her jewellery to her sister's to prevent her husband getting his hands on it.

When he visited his family in Wolverhampton he boasted of how successful he was and flashed a £50 note which would certainly have come from the sale of Ellen's shares.

The violence increased in frequency and intensity over time. While they were lodging with Elizabeth Haynes at Swaton Road she heard Ellen screaming and when she went to investigate she saw Bury crouched over his wife, clutching a knife in his hand. Elizabeth Haynes threatened to call the police but he pleaded with her not to, saying he would never attack Ellen again.

Bury sometimes slept with a knife below his pillow, which may have been because he was frightened of men such as Martin chasing him for money he owed them. Given his background, it is likely that Bury knew some dodgy people and may have had several enemies. Perhaps that was the real reason behind the couple suddenly leaving London.

All of this meant that Ellen probably had good reason to be afraid of her husband and she took the key of their room to Elizabeth Haynes each night, saying she was fearful that he would lock her in and murder her.

The arguments were invariably about money and, when Elizabeth later testified in court, she said she had never seen him sober.

Later, the couple lodged with a bricklayer and builder by the name of William Smith, who also said that Bury was a drunk who ill-treated his wife regularly.

Before the couple left London, Bury asked Smith to make him a large wooden box, three feet by two-feet-six-inches and three-feet deep. This made Smith suspicious but when he asked what it was for he was told that the couple were emigrating to Australia.

But Bury had an entirely different idea in mind. Whether or not he had any sort of plan is unclear but it is possible that in his befuddled state he had already decided to murder Ellen.

He produced a letter, ostensibly from Malcolm, Ogilvy & Co. Ltd, jute spinners and manufacturers in Dundee, offering him employment at £2 per week and his wife at £1 per week. The letter was poorly written and contained numerous errors but, given Ellen's limited education, it did the trick and the couple, having told everyone they were off to Australia, sailed to Dundee on the *SS Cambria*. They arrived in Dundee (**15**) on Sunday 20 January 1889 but didn't disembark until the following day.

Once in Dundee the couple rented rooms at 43 Union Street but within days, they, or more likely Bury, decided that the rent was too high. Bury got keys from a letting agent to look at 'a sunk flat of two rooms' (a basement flat) at 113 Princes Street and moved in. He kept the keys and made no attempt to pay any rent.

Quite how Bury explained the fact that he had no employment lined up isn't clear, although he would no doubt have had some glib explanation and the cowed Ellen was probably too afraid to ask anyway. Nevertheless, he did approach the Rev Edward Gough of St John's Episcopal Church regarding possible employment. Mr Gough suggested the local shipyards might have vacancies but there was, of course, no chance of Bury taking on anything remotely resembling work.

18 *Other than the tram, this Dundee scene would have been familiar to William Bury*

Although the couple probably had little money left by then, Bury managed to spend the next couple of weeks drinking with a number of new acquaintances in a nearby public house. (Shares to the value of £194 had been sold in June 1888 and one of the parties, presumably Ellen, had withdrawn £3 from the bank some eight or nine days before they left London. After the trial it was revealed that the police search of the Princes Street flat had uncovered a bank book, again no doubt the property of Ellen, with a balance of a few pounds in it.)

As well as a pub there was also a small shop at 125 Princes Street, owned by Mrs Janet Martin. On Monday 4 February Bury had gone into the shop and asked if she had a short length of rope. Offered a suitable piece of cord by Mrs Martin he announced 'it would do nicely'. That evening the couple went out drinking. Bury, as ever, returned home drunk while Ellen was relatively sober.

In the early hours of Tuesday, David Duncan, who lived at 101 Princes Street, about twenty-five yards away, was awakened by three loud screams. They were loud enough for him to waken his 'landlady' but she had heard nothing. Duncan listened for around half-an-hour but hearing no further noise he went back to bed.

Another neighbour, Mary Lee, noticed that the blind at the back room window, which had been up during the first week the couple had lived there, was permanently down from that date onward. She was also aware that from that time Bury locked the door whenever he went out, even although Ellen would still have been in the flat. The truth was that she was dead by that time and he couldn't have anyone going in and finding her body.

Bury continued to act much as had done before, spending his time drinking with his new acquaintances. Anyone who asked after Ellen was told that she was at home as she was unwell.

On Sunday 10 February, he went to meet a painter called David Walker at his house. Finding Walker still in bed he picked up a newspaper and started to read it. Walker casually said,

> Look and see if there's anything about Jack the Ripper, you that knows the place.

The remark obviously stung Bury who immediately threw the paper down. Whether the remark hit home or not events moved swiftly from that point.

That evening, Lieutenant Parr was the senior officer on duty at the desk in the Central Police Station in Dundee when, just before seven

19 *Lieutenant Parr, the first police officer to interview William Bury*

20 *Detective Campbell was one of the first police officers to visit the crime scene*

o'clock, an extremely agitated William Bury went in and demanded to speak privately to an officer. Parr thought the man was sober and took him to an interview room but as Bury poured out his harrowing and gruesome tale he began to have second thoughts.

Early on in their conversation Bury apparently said to Parr, 'I am Jack the Ripper' or 'I am a Jack the Ripper'. The difference is crucial but, probably assuming he was dealing with a time-waster rather than a murderer, the Lieutenant decided not to follow up the remark.

Parr's initial reaction was that Bury was deranged and his first few questions were aimed more at assessing the man's mental condition than conducting a murder inquiry. However, as the Englishman poured out his horrific tale Parr quickly realised that he was indeed dealing with a murder.

Bury's story was that on the evening of Monday 4 February the couple had gone out drinking and returned, both very much the worse for wear, he wasn't exactly sure of the time. When he woke up the following morning he found his wife dead, with a rope around her neck.

Having made certain that she was dead he had then, completely on impulse he said, picked up a large knife and set about mutilating the body by stabbing it repeatedly in the abdomen.

It was only when he calmed down that he realised he had to conceal the corpse and he put it in the large wooden box and then put the lid on it, although he left two boards in the centre loose so that they could be lifted off quite easily.

Parr subsequently detained the suspect and advised his superior officers of what he had been told. Lieutenant Lamb, chief of the detective department, then went with Detective Campbell to the address Bury had given. They entered the flat without much difficulty and found the front room completely empty.

In the back room they found a bed and a substantial white wooden box in the middle of the floor, just as Bury had described. On removing the lid and a piece of sheeting they saw the foot and leg of a female. Without disturbing the crime scene any further they locked up and placed an officer on duty outside before reporting their find to the police surgeon.

Dr Templeman arrived shortly afterwards and proceeded to carry out a thorough examination of the box and its contents.

The body had been carefully packed among items of clothing, books, papers etc., but, because it was too large, one of the legs had been bent and the other broken and twisted to get the corpse into the confines of the box. Further examination of the body revealed six or seven stab-wounds on the abdomen, one so deep that part of the deceased's bowel was protruding.

It seemed clear that Mrs Bury had been murdered and Bury was detained on suspicion of murdering his wife.

In custody, Bury gave his full name as William Henry Bury and consented to be searched. On his person, he had just twelve or thirteen shillings (60 or 65p) in change and several items of jewellery, including a watch which he said was one of a number belonging to his late wife. By the standards of the time he seemed rather better-off than his circumstances might have suggested and that, coupled with the fact he could give no good reason why he had come to Dundee, aroused suspicions so the Metropolitan Police were contacted to see if they knew anything about the mysterious Mr Bury.

Now in 1888–89 the whole country was aghast at the murders committed by Jack the Ripper and the newspapers had made the most of the Ripper killings so that few people, even in Scotland, hadn't heard of the shadowy mass murderer.

According to the newspaper reports on the Princes Street crime-scene there was no grate in the fireplace and several window panes were broken, all of which added to the 'dirty and squalid' description of the location.

A full search of the property by the police had revealed a bloodstained knife with flesh and hair on it and a piece of rope with strands of hair entwined around it. The hair appeared to match that of the dead woman.

In the fireplace they also found the charred remains of what was believed to be some of the victim's clothing. Among them was a woman's dark brown ulster, a loose overcoat, which was obviously bloodstained and had several holes in it, presumably made by the murder weapon.

Certainly tears and holes in the garment corresponded with the position of the stab marks on the victim's body which seemed to suggest that poor Ellen had been fully-dressed when stabbed. She had then been strangled to keep her from screaming or calling for help.

After her death, she had been stripped and her body washed before her clothing had been burned in the fireplace in a forlorn attempt to destroy the evidence.

The dilapidated flat might have been similar to many murder-scenes of the period but at the foot of the stair at the back of the property was an old door on which someone had chalked; 'Jack Ripper is at the back of this door', while on the central pillar of the stair in the same hand were the words, 'Jack Ripper is in this sellar' (sic).

A report in the *Dundee Advertiser* had suggested, without any evidence to support the claim, that the writing was the work of a boy and that the authorities would therefore give little credence to it. Nevertheless, the fact that the graffiti predated the tragic events of recent days caused upset in the neighbourhood with locals

> alarmed at what they consider proof that the veritable Whitechapel murderer has been living in their midst.

The London inquiry was dealt with by an Inspector Abberline who was part of the team investigating the Ripper murders. Although not particularly interested in Bury – the Met obviously had no real belief that he was Jack – they had looked into the background of the couple and had quickly established that the ill-fated Ellen had come into money and that Bury had probably married her to get his hands on the cash. In the meantime, progress had also been made at the Dundee end of the investigation as the police pieced together the couple's movements in the city.

21 *Sketches of Bury made at his trial*

Bury was tried at the Spring Circuit Court in Dundee on Thursday 28 March 1889 where he entered a plea of Not Guilty.

Initially, the case for the Crown unfolded largely as above but the medical evidence was to prove crucial to the case and might even have led to an acquittal.

After the discovery of the body it had been taken away for further examination by Templeman and Dr Stalker. At the mortuary, contemporary reports refer to it as the deadhouse, they had found 'a deep red mark' round the neck of the deceased and confirmed the extent of the wounds on the abdomen.

Their findings were at odds with Bury's statement as the two medics took the view that little time had elapsed between the strangulation and the stabbing and they even thought that it was possible the victim had still been alive when the mutilation took place.

Dr Templeman told the court that the bruises on the body indicated that a struggle had taken place and he believed that the strangulation was homicidal rather than suicidal. Suicidal strangulation, Templeman argued, was rare, particularly using a rope wound around the neck only once and that in this case, the violence (pressure) had been downwards, outwards and backwards, all of which indicated strangulation rather than hanging.

He also believed that the wound to the head, indicated by a bruise on the left temporal muscle, had been inflicted by a heavy object such as a poker. A blow of this nature would probably have left the deceased unconscious, or at last partly conscious, either of which would have made it easier to strangle the victim.

Templeman's opinion was that the stab-wounds wouldn't necessarily have induced death but might easily have resulted in death due to shock, particularly in view of Ellen's poor physical condition.

Dr Stalker concurred with his colleague's testimony.

So crucial was the medical evidence to the Crown case that they had also had the body examined by Dr Henry Littlejohn, an Edinburgh police surgeon with many years of experience, who told the Court he believed that the blow to the head had rendered the victim unconscious before she had been strangled and stabbed. In his opinion strangulation and stabbing had been the composite cause of death.

The importance of the medical evidence meant that the only hope the defence had was to show inconsistencies in the testimonies of the expert witnesses. Mr Hay, the advocate appearing for Bury, did his best in his cross-examinations but made no breakthrough likely to help his client escape the ultimate penalty.

Hay did have a legal ace, or two to be exact, up his sleeve however in the form of two doctors willing to speak positively about the possibility that Ellen Bury had committed suicide.

The first medical man to enter the witness box was Dr Lennox, a local doctor who had been in practice for nine years. He testified that, in his opinion, self-strangulation had occurred. More worrying for the Crown was his assertion that the wounds on the body had been inflicted post-mortem i.e. after death.

Lennox was followed by a Dr Kinnear who agreed that suicide by strangulation did occur, although he admitted it was extremely rare. Unfortunately for Bury, Kinnear, under cross-examination, had to admit that he had been in practice for less than six months, a revelation that rather diluted the quality of his testimony.

The Advocate-Depute for the Crown argued that Bury saw Scotland as a sort of lawless place where murder was commonplace and therefore could be committed without anyone taking any notice. He questioned whether Ellen Bury had committed suicide and whether the mutilation of the body had taken place after she was already dead.

In his address to the jury Mr Hay suggested that the bruises on Ellen Bury's body might be explained by her having drunk too much and perhaps fallen down the stairs to the basement. He also debunked the medical evidence given on behalf of the Crown, suggesting that self-strangulation was possible before saying that if indeed his client was guilty then he could have paid two week's rent and been long gone by the time the authorities discovered the body.

In a speech lasting some seventy-five minutes Lord Young said the question before the jury was simply whether or not they believed Ellen Bury had committed suicide or been murdered.

The jury appeared to have little doubt, taking only twenty minutes to find Bury Guilty but they recommended mercy.

Given the violent nature of the murder, this rider to the verdict perplexed Lord Young who inquired as to the jury's reasons for such a recommendation. The answer was,

Partly on the ground of the conflicting medical evidence.

Unhappy with the response, Lord Young sent the jury out to think again and they returned just five minutes later with a Guilty verdict. Satisfied with the outcome Lord Young donned the black cap and delivered the prescribed sentence.

In what was the first hanging in Dundee following the abolition of public hanging Bury was executed on Wednesday 24 April 1889, with the execution following a similar pattern to the others already described in this book.

The prisoner, after partaking of a light breakfast consisting of tea, poached eggs, butter and bread, seemed reconciled to his fate, although the remark that he forgave all those who had given false evidence against him, may have been a sign that he was perhaps still unwilling to accept what he had done.

James Berry from Bradford pulled the lever just as the Rev E J Gough, the man Bury had approached about getting work, finished his prayers.

Bury was five-feet-three-inches tall and weighed ten stones for which Berry had calculated a drop of six-feet-six-inches was required.

His calculations must have been accurate as, although the body was allowed to hang for an hour before being taken down and life pronounced to be extinct, the prison surgeon, Dr Millar, who later examined the body, confirmed that death had resulted from the fracture of the spinal column and had been instantaneous. The body was placed in a rough deal coffin and interred in quicklime in the prison grounds that evening.

At 10:00 am there was a formal inquest at the Sheriff Court House where the Prison Governor reported that Mr Gough had asked him to intimate that the accused had left a written confession which confirmed that he had strangled and then stabbed his victim, just as the medical evidence had suggested.

William Bury was probably little more than a violent and drunken conman whose greed caused him to murder his first and, as far as we know, only victim, his wife Ellen. We know too that William was bone-idle but was he the Ripper?

Certainly the case has been made, albeit somewhat circumstantially. It has been suggested that the Ripper murders appeared to stop after his execution but there were at least two subsequent murders that might have been perpetrated by the Ripper.

In truth, the argument that Bury was Jack doesn't really stand up. Jack had come stealthily in the night, selecting his victim, or perhaps just picking on some lowly lady of the night at random, but he always covered his tracks well. Bury on the other hand seems to have been little more than a ham-fisted opportunist.

He may have had some sort of plan, for example ordering the wooden box and travelling to Dundee, but other than that he seems to have been clueless. If he had murdered Ellen just after arriving in Dundee he could have fled back to London or even further afield. No one would have known who she was and it is likely he would have escaped scot-free.

This lack of planning, other than the purchase of the length of cord, was obvious from his conduct after the murder. He may have intended to murder Ellen at some point, presumably after he had all her money, but it seems likely that he acted on the spur of the moment.

The act was probably committed in a drunken rage during an argument about money and it was only then that he had realised the problems of getting rid of the body and making good his escape.

The Ripper's mutilation of the bodies was different too (he invariably cut his victim's throats and often removed body parts), but, even allowing for that, would the real Jack have gone to the police to confess? It seems unlikely.

22 *Another sketch of Bury that was published in the newspapers of the day*

Bury's mother died in a lunatic asylum when he was quite young so perhaps he too had mental problems which, aggravated by his heavy drinking, had made him delusional. In fact, Bury did make a verbal confession of sorts to his law agent and the contents were published in the press on Friday 26 April. According to his 'confession', both parties were the worse for wear through drink on the night of 4 February. (There is no evidence that Ellen Bury had drunk much if anything and an analysis of her stomach contents after her murder had not indicated the presence of alcohol.)

She had made 'certain suggestions' about him finding work but her proposals had so angered him that he grabbed the piece of cord (that he had so conveniently obtained that very day) and strangled her.

When he awoke from his drunken sleep the following morning he realised what he had done. His first thought was that he could dispose of the body by cutting it up and disposing of the pieces, 'bit by bit' in the Tay but, as he hacked away at the body, he was sickened and unable to continue.

He then forced the remains into the large wooden box with the intention of having it collected by porters and forwarded by rail to London to be called for. Despite the problems of sending a decomposing body on such a journey his argument against this course of action was simply that the neighbours might be suspicious of the fact that his wife had disappeared.

Having failed to come up with anything else he

> spent a miserable week beside the body, and was in such a state of remorse of conscience that on the Sunday evening he surrendered to the police, to whom he invented the story of his wife's suicide, hoping that in that way he might deceive them and escape.

It has also been suggested that Bury made a second, more detailed, confession which was forwarded to the Home Secretary. Although this document was never made public it apparently contained some startling revelations about the Whitechapel murders. That, coupled with the 'fact' that the murders stopped around the time of his execution, gave rise to the theory that Bury was The Ripper.

In fact, Bury's sawdust business would have taken him to places where gossip and rumours about the murders would have abounded, perhaps giving him an apparent knowledge of some of the grislier elements of the crimes.

I believe that a man as conceited and boastful as Bury would have taken the 'credit' of being the Ripper if he was in fact the mass murderer.

Like Robertson, his grave was marked by a simple stone, this one in the courtyard of the Old Jail of Dundee. It read 'W H B 24.4.1889'.

1889   Joseph Redmond

On Saturday 30 March, even as the citizens of Dundee awaited the execution of William Berry, there was another horrific murder in the city.

The victim in this case was Bridget Jenkins or Redmond, who kept a small grocer's shop on St Mary Street, just off Lochee Road.

Bridget Redmond was thought to be about forty-five years old and had lived in the street for some fifteen years and had been the occupant of the shop from the time the tenement had been built. Joseph Redmond, a former soldier, was about two years older than his wife. They had married eleven years before and the shop had been transferred into his name

The couple were both Roman Catholics and attended St Joseph's Chapel in Dundee. Financially, they appeared to be reasonably well off, the business was sound and Joseph was in receipt of a good pension. They owned another property in Lochee Road and were thought to have been considering retirement and taking up residence there.

Bridget was described as a 'very decent, quiet, sober, steady woman' but her husband apparently had a violent temper and was prone to fits of rage. He was over-fond of drink and, on occasion, that had led to problems in the relationship.

Just before noon, Mrs Redmond had been standing outside the shop speaking to a neighbour when Charles Anderson, a vanman with one of the local bakers, arrived to make his daily delivery.

Mrs Redmond went back into the shop and at about the same time, a little girl, Maggie McHardy, also went into the shop on an errand for her mother. Just as Mrs Redmond was serving the girl, her husband, Joseph Redmond, came into the shop.

He ignored his wife and young customer but remarked to Anderson that it was 'a fine day' before making his way behind the counter where he lifted up a large knife used for cutting ham and cheese. As Mrs Redmond bent to get some onions out of a bag he plunged the knife twice into her upper back. Anderson, on hearing the noise, turned and saw Redmond holding the knife. He quickly disarmed Redmond who simply stood there without uttering a word.

Mrs Redmond staggered out of the shop, asking neighbours to take her in. Thomas Burke, a local coal-merchant, took her by the arm and led her towards his house but she collapsed before reaching it and died about twenty-five minutes later without regaining consciousness.

Redmond, still standing outside the shop calmly smoking his pipe, was apprehended within minutes. Seeing two constables approaching, he took the shop keys out of his pocket and locked the door. Told that he would be charged with murder he replied, 'Oh! Is she dead?'

He was taken to the police office where he was formally charged. Perhaps by this time he realised what he had done for his response was

> Poor Bridget, poor Bridget, I could be hanged tomorrow if it would bring you back to life.

One neighbour, a Mrs Hutton, said she had spoken to Redmond about the Bury murder. He had obviously followed the reports of the trial very closely and remarked to her that

> hanging was too good for that scoundrel Bury.

Until the murder the Redmonds had apparently lived quite happily together other than his occasional outbursts of violence. He had been in the Army for nineteen years and had spent part of that time serving in India where he suffered from sunstroke. Whether or not this was contributing factor wasn't clear but he was reputed to have shown signs of mental instability on occasions after his discharge.

In fact his medical history prevented him from hanging. When the case came to court in Edinburgh on 29 April 1889 evidence was produced confirming that he had suffered from sunstroke while in India and had from that time suffered from delusions. He was ordered to be confined during Her Majesty's pleasure.

In legal terms much had changed since the execution of Andrew Brown in 1865.

1890   John Webster

As November 1890 drew to a close, rumours began to circulate in the town of Kirriemuir, famous as the birthplace of author J M Barrie, the creator of Peter Pan, that Mary Webster, the wife of local hotel keeper John Webster, who had died on 4 August, had been poisoned. Mary Ann Innes or Webster, aged just thirty-three, had died after being ill for a matter of days and Dr Clark, a local GP, had certified the cause of death as gastritis.

That might have been the end of the matter but it soon came to light that Webster had only recently insured his wife's life for £1,000 with the Prudential Assurance Company and only a couple of premiums had been paid. After making inquiries into Mrs Webster's death the Company had refused to pay out on the policy and, consequently, the Procurator-Fiscal began his own investigation.

It had also been revealed that the couple had separated for a time and Mrs Webster had only resumed living with her husband when he took over the Newton Hotel in the town.

Webster and his wife had been married for about twelve years and the couple had seven children, although only two daughters had survived. They appeared to be happy enough together, although rumour had it that there had been serious problems during the final year of their marriage.

In autumn 1889, Webster had contacted the Prudential with a view to insuring the deceased's life. His explanation was that the couple intended to emigrate and he had heard of people dying on the voyage. The Company's rules wouldn't permit such a policy so the Websters had what is known as a 'double life' policy with the lives of both parties insured.

The premium was almost £25 per half year and the company expressed doubts as to whether or not Webster could afford what was then a considerable sum. He explained that he had carried on a successful business as a cattle dealer so the policy had been issued and the first two premiums paid.

23 *The Newton Hotel, Kirriemuir*

In June 1890, Webster intimated to the Company that he was now resident at the Newton Hotel in Kirriemuir and it was around that time that Mrs Webster, who had been living with her father, returned to live with him.

Between June and the beginning of August she made a number of visits to friends in Dundee when she had intimated that she was not happy in her new life.

Mrs Webster took ill on 1 August. She was confined to bed, although the doctor wasn't called until two days later. When Dr Clark returned on the morning of 4 August he was told she had died and, after viewing the body, he issued a death certificate giving the cause of death as gastritis.

The body, which had been interred in the Eastern Cemetery in Dundee, was exhumed on 27 November to allow a post-mortem to be carried out by Dr Littlejohn from Edinburgh and Dr Clark.

Despite the fact that the whole exercise had been carried out discreetly, rumours soon began circulating in both Kirriemuir and Dundee and John Webster was arrested on the morning of 4 December, charged with murdering his wife by poisoning her.

Trial was set for 16 January 1891 at the High Court of Justiciary in Edinburgh but it was immediately adjourned due to the nonappearance of one of the principal witnesses.

James Peacock, one of the Crown's main witnesses, had failed to appear and inquiries had revealed that he had gone missing from his home in Kirriemuir. The Lord Advocate asked for, and was granted, a warrant for Peacock's arrest.

Peacock had been employed by Webster as a barman at the Newton Hotel where the murder was alleged to have taken place. He had purchased a half mutchkin (almost 1·5 gills or 213 ml) of whisky before he left the hotel on the previous Wednesday, something he was not in the habit of doing as he was said to be of temperate habits. That evening, he left his mother's house where he stayed, saying he was going out to post a letter. He never returned.

There were various theories about his sudden disappearance but the letter he had posted duly arrived, although his savings remained untouched. The most likely theory was that the trial had weighed so heavily on his mind that he had done away with himself.

Searches of the area and the Prosen and Esk Rivers revealed nothing and the authorities approached two of the local textile companies seeking permission to empty their mill ponds when work finished for the week.

The sluice at Wilkie's Kirriemuir Linen Works had only been open for a short time when Peacock's body was spotted lying face down in the water. Among the possessions found on the body was the citation to appear at the High Court and it seemed fairly obvious that he had committed suicide.

It was suggested that Peacock was a fairly important witness and there were fears that the trial might not proceed but that idea was soon put to rest.

But Peacock's suicide wasn't the final twist in the story. On Wednesday 21 January there was another sensational development which compounded the mystery of the murder in 'Thrums' (J M Barrie's fictional town based on Kirriemuir) still further when it was announced that the death of Mrs Donald, the previous owner of the Newton Hotel, was also being investigated.

Mrs Donald had died at the Newton Hotel on 21 March 1890 having been ill for some twenty-nine hours. A widow in her forty-third year, she had hired a new barman, James Peacock, just four days before her death.

Mrs Donald had taken ill on 19 March, complaining of severe pains in her chest and stomach. Despite the attentions of a local doctor her condition had continued to deteriorate. Her death had been put down to peritonitis.

It wasn't thought that Peacock had had any direct contact with her during her illness, although one witness said he had stayed with her during her final hours. Mrs Donald had previously been in good health and, in the light of the murder charge against Webster, her sudden death had raised enough suspicion for the Crown to seek the necessary permission to exhume her body.

When John Webster's trial finally started on 17 February 1891, *The Montrose Review* reported that the case had

> evoked an amount of public interest greater than has been shown in any Scotch criminal prosecution since the trial of Lawrie for the Arran murder, and not far short of that aroused by the trials of the notorious Madeline Smith and Dr Pritchard.

Webster was charged that:

> between 25th July and 5th August, 1890, within the Newton Hotel, Southmuir of Kirriemuir, parish of Kirriemuir, Forfarshire, then occupied by him, he did administer poison to Mary Ann Webster, his wife, and did murder her.

The first witness, Helen Ross Hendry Grant, a domestic servant, confirmed that the deceased had been very ill, often violently sick, with a strong thirst. She also told the court she was never present when medicine was given to Mrs Webster, although she did confirm that it was the accused who had told her to get a doctor and he had said to get an experienced one, not a young man.

Grant also told the court that Mrs Webster's bed-linen was badly stained, the colour of port wine. Mrs Webster had told her the staining was caused by the medicine she was taking.

Arthur King Milne, surgeon, Kirriemuir, said he had examined the body of James Peacock and he had no doubt his death had been suicide. The following witness, Frederick Alexander Johnston was a law clerk in Kirriemuir. He said he could shed some light on why Peacock had committed suicide. On 11 January he had had a conversation with Peacock who asked what would happen if the evidence given by a witness differed markedly from his previous statement.

Mr Johnston said he would require to explain himself and asked why he was so concerned. Peacock had replied that he had told the Fiscal that he had never heard Mrs Webster vomiting but afterwards recalled that he had.

Another thing that worried him was the fact that when the Fiscal asked him how the accused looked when he knew his wife was dead he hadn't been able to answer and the fiscal had written something down. He then told the witness that the accused had looked like any man hearing about the death of his wife or a dear friend but he hadn't been able to find words to answer the Fiscal.

The witness had told him he should just tell the truth but he felt that Peacock seemed more alarmed than an ordinary man would have been about his forgetfulness.

Johnston was followed by Elizabeth Webster, the eleven-year-old daughter of the accused, whose most important piece of evidence, considering what was to come, was that she thought her mother and father were quite happy together.

Dr Clark, who had attended the deceased in her last days, explained that she had been pale, weak and exhausted, complaining of pain in her stomach and suffering from severe thirst but had little appetite.

Having attended the patient again on Sunday 3 August and prescribed treatment, he said he was surprised to see her no better the following day. He confirmed that he had given gastritis as the cause of death.

Another witness, police-sergeant Clark of Kirriemuir, confirmed that he had removed several bottles that the accused had advised contained the medicines taken by the deceased. John Forsyth, chemist, Dundee said he had made up sixty pills for the deceased, some of which contained poisonous ingredients. He admitted that it was possible that phosphate of iron and another ingredient might have been

> slightly contaminated with arsenic, but the quantity, even in sixty pills, would have been unappreciable.

It was the evidence of the next witness, Dr Littlejohn, Medical Officer of Health for Edinburgh, who had carried out the post-mortem along with Dr Clark, that those in the packed courtroom were waiting to hear. Littlejohn's evidence was initially damning.

The first examination had shown no obvious cause of death so they had removed parts of the body for chemical examination. They had looked particularly at the large organs but could find no disease.

After that, they had examined the lining of the stomach and found nothing odd about it other than a yellow patch on the surface of the stomach and dark coloured mucous inside. Dr Littlejohn felt it was surprising that this congestion should still be present so long after death.

He removed the mucous matter and proceeded to wash and soak it in distilled water. Analysis using the Reinsch test, which had replaced the Marsh test, indicated the presence of arsenic.

On finding arsenic in the stomach he had immediately advised the Crown of the fact and was instructed to work with Mr Falconer King in making further examinations.

It was, he said, well known that the presence of arsenic meant that the body remained well preserved even after burial and he also pointed out that the arsenic could only be accounted for by having been there when Mrs Webster was still alive.

Having made this discovery they performed further analysis which allowed them to calculate the amount of arsenic present in the stomach as being almost five grains of arsenic trioxide, commonly known as white arsenic. Other organs showed traces of arsenic but in smaller quantities. Given the evidence of the deceased's vomiting as she neared death it was likely that the final dose would have been 'thrown off'.

All the evidence pointed to arsenic having been regularly and recently administered to the deceased. He could say that it was recent because he had found it in the stomach and he could also say it had been administered regularly because it appeared in other, more distant, organs.

This all fitted with the deceased's symptoms. Severe vomiting, great thirst and stomach pains were characteristic of arsenical poisoning, although the symptoms could vary from person to person.

The deceased's liver had fatty degeneration, another characteristic of arsenical poisoning, although the condition could indicate heavy drinking but, in this instance, the examination of other organs meant that he could exclude that possibility.

He agreed that arsenic was a possible impurity in phosphate of iron but was surprised to hear that any chemist of the time would keep it anywhere where it might be contaminated by arsenic.

Death would have resulted from the two grains of arsenic identified (half the amount given in his initial report) in the analysis carried out with Mr King, although he pointed out that the arsenic that killed wasn't necessarily the poison found after death.

Dr Littlejohn was skilfully cross-examined by Mr Asher QC for the defence. The witness agreed that he would have expected to find a number of spontaneous changes brought about by decomposition but felt he was experienced enough to identify those as distinct from the changes caused by the poison.

Counsel read from a textbook on jurisprudence which pointed out that putrefaction might easily be mistaken for the effects of poisoning. Littlejohn agreed there were no set rules to guide practitioners and that in some cases arsenic brought about rapid decomposition while it was much slower in other instances as many external factors were involved.

Mr Asher then introduced the subject of our old friend Fowler's Solution, the patent medicine available from any chemist, and he asked the witness how many grains of arsenic there were in an ounce of the solution.

The witness thought four, although he bowed to counsel's knowledge that there were 4·5. He said two tablespoonfuls of the medicine, which was dark red in colour like a dark sherry, would be about an ounce.

Yes, he had to agree that the arsenic in the organs examined by him might have been taken into the body in the form of Fowler's Solution. He also accepted that the greatest care had to be taken in dealing with the amount of arsenic found in a body and he admitted that the quantity (five grains) given in his first report was wrong. There was no doubt that arsenic was present but there was uncertainty about the amount. He could exclude death from disease of either the kidneys or heart.

In conclusion Dr Littlejohn said that no Fowler's Solution had been found in any of the bottles removed from the accused's premises.

Dr Clark was recalled and confirmed that irrespective of the cause the correct name for the complaint was inflammation of the stomach, in other words gastritis, although he agreed that patients rarely died from ordinary gastritis.

That completed the proceedings for the day. The jury were sent to an hotel but asked not to discuss the case as they had heard only part of the evidence.

The first witness on the following day was Dr J Falconer King, Edinburgh City analyst, who corroborated the evidence given by Dr Littlejohn. He also explained that he had been responsible for analysing the various packets and bottles removed from the accused's hotel and confirmed that, other than one which contained a minute trace of arsenic, he found no other sign of the poison.

Cross-examined by Mr Asher, he confirmed that the final report gave the amount of arsenic in the organs as 0·71.

The next witness was Professor Crum Brown who explained how the analytical examination had been carried out. He said that arsenic had been found in every organ examined by him and said the total amount found in the organs and weighed by him amounted to 0·273 while the semi-fluid matter from the stomach had yielded the most arsenic. Under cross-examination he gave the revised amount of arsenic in the stomach as 1·75 grains.

The problems that had arisen between the accused and the deceased were largely explained by the suggestion, although it was not spelt out in any detail, that Webster believed she had passed on a sexually transmitted disease to him. A number of witnesses attested to Mrs Webster's physical condition but the most telling evidence came from Dr David Lennox who had examined the couple in October 1889 with regard to their application for a life policy.

In the following summer Mrs Webster had consulted him again, complaining of

> a strange feeling in the lower part of her stomach, accompanied by abdominal discharges.

He prescribed various medicines for her but said none contained arsenic. From her symptoms he believed the discharge was probably chronic and thought it might be transmitted to her husband which in fact it had been. He had reassured the accused that the discharge didn't reflect in the slightest on his wife's moral character.

The other possible cause of conflict was that Mrs Webster had changed her mind about emigrating but whether or not this was ever a serious option we cannot be certain.

The accused's declaration, in which he denied the charge, was read to the court before the defence case was presented.

An indication of Mrs Webster's health problems was given by the accused's sister, Jessie Webster, who explained that she had stayed with the family during which time she had shared a bed with the deceased.

She had noticed that the deceased slept in her petticoat, a habit she assumed to prevent further soiling of the bedclothes. In addition, she told the court that the deceased's breath smelt terrible and it was so revolting she could scarcely share the same bed.

The deceased obviously had physical problems and she had warned the witness not to use her 'bedroom vessel', presumably the chamber pot, as it was dangerous and also announced that she felt so bad she was going to consult a doctor in Dundee.

Miss Webster also confirmed that she saw two medicine bottles in the room, although she never saw the deceased taking any. One of the bottles contained a dark liquid, similar to the colour of brown sherry. She said that the deceased had been sick on a number of occasions during her stay.

The defence had its own medical experts too and Dr R Murray Milne of Edinburgh said he had inspected the deceased's uterus and from that he thought she might have suffered from 'sub-involution' (the term for the failure of the womb to return to its normal size after childbirth), which would have explained her symptoms. He told the court that arsenic was commonly used as a remedy for the complaint.

His colleague, Dr Bruce, who had assisted him, was 'emphatic' that after the body had been interred for four months it was impossible to say whether the fatty degeneration of the liver was due to arsenical poisoning or natural decomposition.

Another witness, Professor Fraser of Edinburgh University, confirmed the possibility of sub-involution being a factor and he spoke at length of the use of Fowler's Solution of arsenic. He said, it looked not unlike sherry, was easily obtained and very agreeable to take. A lethal dose might not take effect for several days, possibly seven, ten or even thirteen days, and four to six grains would be a lethal dose.

He confirmed the view about the risks of making deductions from the state of the liver where a body had been buried for four months. Finally, he pointed out that arsenic was a common means of committing suicide.

The Solicitor-General then addressed the jury. He argued that there seemed little doubt that the deceased had been poisoned which only left the question of how that had happened. Either, she had died by misadventure, the cause of her own death through overdosing on her medication, or 'death by design' as a result of suicide or murder. There was no evidence of suicide and, if death wasn't accidental and wasn't suicide, then it had to murder.

The only question remaining was who had administered the arsenic? He felt they could exclude Peacock, whose death had been explained and the serving-girl Grant, which only left the accused.

There were two possible motives; the couple had latterly had a strained relationship and, of course, on her death, the accused stood to gain £1,000.

After a break for lunch it was Mr Asher's turn to deliver his address to the jury. It was a moving address, delivered in a quiet but impressive manner, to the jury. He dwelt on the circumstantial elements of the evidence, pointed out that the medical experts had been unable to agree and said that, despite the allegations of disharmony, it had been clearly shown in evidence that his client had been visibly upset at the death of his wife.

One factor, which he described as unique in such a case, was that no attempt had been made to prove that the accused had ever been in possession of arsenic.

He closed his speech with 'an infusion of mingled passion and pathos' and, as he described the scene between Webster and his little daughter in the bedroom, alone with the dead woman, the prisoner gave way again and wept unrestrainedly.

Addressing the jury, the Lord Justice Clerk said the initial report produced by the prosecution's expert witnesses had been 'seriously incorrect'. He also repeated Mr Asher's remarks about there being no evidence that Webster had obtained arsenic or had any in his possession before finishing by saying that

> in spite of all the quarrels and bitter things that must have been said the wife never lost her affection for him.

The prosecution case was doomed and it took the jury just eight minutes to bring in a unanimous verdict of Not Guilty.

On 5 March, an action by John Webster against the Prudential Assurance Company was disposed of and the outstanding sum, along with interest and expenses, was paid over.

Following the exhumation of Mary Webster's body, a docket was added to the back of her death certificate, although the cause of death, 'gastritis', is the same as that shown originally. Irrespective of whether she was deliberately poisoned or whether it was self-inflicted the outcome was the same.

A Taste For Killing

A final local story from an earlier period that will chill the blood —

On the east side of road between Monikie and Newbigging is a farm called Denfind, formerly Dunfind.

A few hundred yards south of the current farm entrance, on the same side of the road, is a valley all but hidden from view. A small burn, crossed by an arched bridge over the road, meanders through the valley which, in bygone days, must have been an excellent place of concealment.

That was the use it was put to by the family of robbers who dwelt there. Not only did they rob unwary travellers but they also subdued them before taking them back to their lair and eating them. Such was the family's taste for human flesh that they believed that the younger their victim the more tender, and so more enjoyable, the flesh.

Inevitably, the law finally caught up with the cannibal family and other than the youngest daughter, a lass of about a year old, they were all executed by burning.

The youngster was taken to Dundee where she was brought up in a civilised manner but the taste for human flesh was obviously in her genes and when she reached adulthood she too began to kill and eat her victims.

She was also brought to justice and her execution was attended by a huge crowd, many of them women.

As she was subjected to the anger of the masses gathered to see her burn she told them,

> Why chide ye me as if I had committed a crime. Give me credit, if ye had the experience of eating human flesh ye would think it so delicious that you would never forbear it again.

The valley is now called Denfiend!

— and a couple of tales that have nothing to do with Angus or Dundee but are certainly worth telling.

Hanged Until Dead

1724 — Margaret Dickson

The first is of a fish-seller called Margaret Dickson. Apparently she was deserted by her husband in 1723 and, having a living to make, she moved to Kelso where she found work at a local inn. According to the tale she became pregnant, probably having dallied with either the innkeeper or his son.

Whether the child had been born dead or whether she did away with it is unclear but, leaving the question of infanticide aside, it was still a capital offence to conceal a pregnancy and birth.

In a male-dominated society, the apparently luckless Margaret was tried, found guilty and hanged on 2 September 1724. Margaret was cut down and pronounced dead. End of story – well not quite.

As the corpse was being taken away in a coffin noises were heard. The coffin was opened up and a rather bewildered Margaret was found to be alive.

The legal view was that as she had been hanged she couldn't be hanged again so that was the end of the matter, except that she became known as 'Half Hangit Maggie' and enjoyed her celebrity status for at least forty more years.

1818 — Matthew Clydesdale

The other tale, which concerns the hanging of a murderer called Matthew Clydesdale, is even more bizarre.

Two men were hanged in Glasgow on 4 November 1818. Simon Ross was hanged for housebreaking while Clydesdale was hanged for the apparently motiveless murder of an old man near Clarkston.

Now the body of Ross was given to his relatives but, because he was a murderer, Clydesdale's corpse was destined for the anatomy department at the University of Glasgow where Professors Andrew Ure and James Jaffray were waiting.

In 1818 electricity was seen as having almost magical powers and the possibility of being able to restore life was just one of the many theories that scientists were looking to investigate. So, instead of Clydesdale's body being sent simply for dissection, it was to be the guinea-pig for a new ground-breaking experiment.

Galvanism, the use of electric current to stimulate the human body, was seen as a great scientific breakthrough and the professors intended to subject the Clydesdale's body to a series of electric shocks and record the results.

Just over thirty years later, the idea that Clydesdale had actually been restored to life gained ground after being recounted in *Reminiscences of Glasgow and the West of Scotland* by Peter Mackenzie and then repeated in *Glasgow's Story* by C Stewart Black many years later. A bit like the Clydesdale myth the story took on a life of its own.

There had been rumours that some of Clydesdale's fellow miners would make a rescue attempt so the scaffold was guarded by men of the 40th Regiment of Foot, bolstered by the presence of a detachment of the 1st Dragoon Guards.

Clydesdale was duly despatched to meet his maker by executioner Thomas Young and the body transferred to a cart which, accompanied by the soldiers, made its way to the college and to the anatomy lecture room. The corpse was still fully dressed and after the white hood and the bonds had been removed it was placed in an easy chair.

Before a packed theatre of eager students and members of the public, Ure proceeded to produce different effects such as smiles and grimaces, make fingers move and even temporarily restore breathing but not, despite some reports, to restore life itself.

But, according to Black,

> An air tube, connected to bellows, was put in one of his nostrils, and the galvanic battery was applied to his arms ... His chest heaved, his eyelids struggled apart, and wild eyes glared between them ... The dead had come to life.

This raised an interesting problem. If Clydesdale came back to life he would presumably, under Scots Law, having paid the price, been a free man. In Black's account the matter was quickly resolved by Jaffray who, whether fearful for his reputation if the murderer survived because of his experiment or simply because he wasn't inclined to lose his 'anatomical specimen', drew a lancet from his pocket and cut Clydesdale's carotid artery, bringing the ghastly saga to an end.

Black's view was that, like Half Hangit Maggie, Clydesdale had been subjected to 'ineffective strangulation'.

In fact Ure and Jaffray's experiments had involved making incisions in Clydesdale's body so that it was drained of blood and the hanging, whether or not it had been completely effective, had severely damaged the spine.

The Glasgow rumour-mill however had no doubts and the word on the streets was simple; Clydesdale had walked and talked and had it not been for the intervention of Jaffray, would have been resurrected.

It is possible that if Clydesdale had been the subject of 'ineffective strangulation' then he could have been brought back to life because what Ure and Jaffray had effectively done was invent the defibrillator. The truth however is that Clydesdale died on the scaffold.

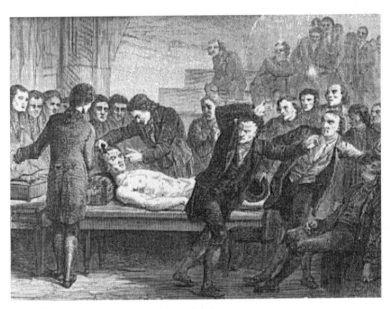

24 *The grisly experiment on Clydesdale's corpse*

The Hangmen

In the sixteenth century most burghs employed an executioner, or at least someone whose duty it was to administer punishment. Executions weren't perhaps as regular as we might believe but there was still plenty for the executioner to do as he was expected to carry out sentences such as lugging (cutting off an ear), scourging or whipping, branding and putting offenders in the stocks.

Hangmen had several nicknames. Possibly the most obvious was 'hangie', not to be confused with 'Auld Hangie', which was one of many such names for the Devil.

Other names for the executioner included lockman or lokman, basar or burrio. The term staffman sometimes referred to an official, such as a constable who carried a staff or badge of office, but could also mean the burgh hangman.

The dempster or doomster was responsible for pronouncing sentence or doom as laid down by the judge and that task was also part of the executioner's duties in earlier times.

The terms lokman/lockman was derived from one of the hangman's perks; the right to a lock or handful of all produce brought into the market place. In the early days, the executioner was often given a suit of clothes or a uniform and other allowances, including payment in kind – such as being supplied with coal or peat, a bed and bedding and even a house – in addition to an annual salary and payment for each execution. An indication of payment, where known, has been given in the relevant part of the text.

Frequently, the hangman was himself a convicted criminal, who took on the job in order to escape the noose.

Eventually, the smaller burghs realised that they didn't require an executioner and they dispensed with the post to save money. This trend continued until there were only hangmen in the major cities and then finally one or two executioners covered the whole country, paid each time they carried out their grisly work.

The appointment of an executioner was marked by a bizarre ceremony. He was taken into the council chambers where an axe, a pair of leg-irons, handcuffs, a short length of rope and a pair of white caps had been set out on the table.

As he knelt in front of the table he repeated the oath:

> I swear to hang, or behead, and to draw, or quarter, or otherwise destroy
> all felons or enemies to the peace of our Lord the King, and his subjects
> duly sentenced according to law, and I will do the like unto father, or
> mother, sister, or brother, and all kindred whatsoever. So help me God.

The oath completed, a black cloth was thrown over him as he rose and
he was led from the building as the assembled crowd groaned, the dead-
bell tolled and with the magistrate's final words, 'Get thee hence
wretch', ringing in his ear.

Many hangmen took to drink later in their lives but whether this was
a coping mechanism or simply because they were liberally treated by
those hoping to hear tales of their appalling craft isn't clear. In truth
there may have been a measure of both, although hangmen weren't
universally popular so popping into their local for a pint wasn't really
a safe option.

Isaac Gibbs (prisoner Patrick Ogilvie)

Apparently an ex-soldier, Gibbs was appointed as Edinburgh City
executioner on 10 December 1762 but resigned in December 1765, just
weeks after his inefficient showing at the execution of Patrick Ogilvie.
We will never know whether or not the two events were linked.

James Chapman (Andrew Low?)

In his account of the Low case, Lowson uses the first name James at
one point in the text and later uses the name John, although he seems
clear that the executioner was from Aberdeen. Little is known of
Chapman other than that he acted as executioner in the case of
Alexander Cheyne at Aberdeen in 1748.

Robert Welsh (Andrew Low)

In *Young's Encyclopaedia of Scottish Executions* Welsh is given as the
executioner of Andrew Low and the surviving records suggest that
this is more likely.

The post of hangman in Aberdeen had been vacant for some time before
Welsh was appointed in 1773. His initial salary was thirteen shillings
and four pence (67p) per month but this had risen to twenty-one
shillings and seven pence (£1.08) by 1800.

The hangman in the execution of Margaret Tindal or Shuttleworth was certainly John Milne as there is correspondence from Mr Cadenhead, Aberdeen's Procurator Fiscal, to the authorities in Montrose about engaging him for the task.

Having spoken to Milne, Cadenhead confirmed that he was willing to undertake the job and, as far as cost was concerned, would be looking for £10, as he had been paid that for a visit 'to Forfar on a similar occasion.' (There is no record of any execution in Forfar between Low in 1785 and Margaret Wishart in 1827 so either he carried out some other, less grisly, duty or he was simply mistaken.)

Like so many of the hangmen, John Milne was a convicted criminal. He had been found guilty in April 1806 of stealing beehives and given the alternative of transportation or taking up the post of hangman with a salary of seven pounds ten shillings (£7.50) for six months.

Although he had an evil reputation, and a shrew of a wife, money doesn't appear to have been a major concern to him.

Mrs Shuttleworth's execution was postponed twice. The second postponement was for one month and Milne had come to Montrose for that date. However it wasn't clear whether the delay referred to a lunar or calendar month so a further five days extension was granted.

Milne was given £2 for his time and trouble in undertaking his fruitless trip to the burgh. He returned to carry out his gruesome task on 7 December but although he was offered the full £10 he would only take £8, the balance due on the original amount.

A later newspaper report, referring to the Shuttleworth execution, reminded readers of the hangman's right to the clothes of his victim as a perk and said that Milne declined to take them that day. A heavy storm had struck the town during the execution and the condemned woman was soaked through. On being offered her clothes the executioner is said to have responded:

Poor thing, she'll be cauld enough even wi her claes; let her gang wi them. In fact the day of the execution was so dark that local people had to have their cruisies (lamps) lit at midday. To a superstitious population this was a sign that God was frowning on the town for executing an innocent woman.

Thomas Williams (Margaret Wishart)

Thomas Williams, the man responsible for the execution of Margaret Wishart, was the Edinburgh hangman, appointed by the Council there in December 1819, although his appointment was not formally confirmed until March of the following year.

In June 1820 he was awarded the doomster's allowance by the Exchequer and given a free house so his weekly wage was reduced from fourteen to twelve shillings per week. This represents a salary of just over £31 per annum, although, like his fellows, he would have been paid separately for his work elsewhere.

William Calcraft (Andrew Brown)

William Calcraft, the executioner of Andrew Brown, was the first celebrity hangman. Initially, Calcraft was one of the street-traders who sold food at public hangings but he decided that he could execute wrongdoers. He became an assistant hangman at Lincoln and when the opportunity arose he applied for the top job and got it, serving as hangman for London and Middlesex from 1829 until he retired.

As he also traded as a shoemaker he was well rewarded between his day job and his lucrative duties as a hangman.

Before long he became a peripatetic hangman, travelling throughout the country to provide his gruesome services.

Calcraft was the perfect executioner in a professional sense in that he was both cold and detached. His youngest victim was just nine years old and he dispatched some of the most notorious criminals of his day. He is credited with devising a new form of harness for pinioning prisoners and for looking at ways of hastening death, although only by pulling on legs or jumping on prisoners' backs as they struggled for breath at the end of the rope.

In fact, like his predecessors, most of his victims were strangled and, although it has been suggested that he was incompetent, he was simply no better or no worse than any of his compatriots.

Calcraft and his predecessors used a halter-style noose; one end of a single piece of rope was simply fed through a loop which was another part of the same rope. The practice of making a noose and then winding the rope around itself, the method used in all good cowboy films, was rarely, if ever, used in the UK.

William Calcraft announced in April 1873 that he was shortly to retire from public life, 'to seek the repose of cultivating roses, dahlias, and tulips'. The Corporation of London was to pay him an honorarium of £1 per week and a report of the time said it was expected that the Home Office would supplement that amount.

He died, a tragic figure after the loss of his wife and his work, on 13 December 1879.

For the execution of Andrew Brown, Calcraft arrived in Montrose the day before and was accommodated in the Eagle Inn across from the prison, on the site now occupied by the George Hotel.

He remained at the Eagle, leaving only to perform his official duty and when taking his leave of the town, once he had received his fee and expenses which totalled £28.

According to one account Calcraft met up with two women in the Eagle Inn and bought them a drink. They were apparently very taken with the well-mannered gentleman until they discovered his occupation whereupon they were promptly sick.

It is said that Calcraft always took away a personal souvenir of his victims and we can only wonder what he kept as a memento of the day he dispatched the unfortunate Andrew Brown.

He also supplemented his income by selling off pieces of the ropes he used at rates varying between five shillings (25p) to one pound per inch, the price depending on the notoriety of the perpetrator.

James Berry   (William Bury)

Berry was the man charged with executing William Bury at Dundee in 1889. Born in 1852, Berry had tried numerous occupations without success before he applied for the job as hangman after Marwood died, having written in his application that he had consulted him about his approach to the profession.

One of his jobs had been with Bradford police and Berry himself suggested that he felt he was destined to succeed Marwood. Indeed, he wrote in his memoirs:

> It seemed that I was predestined from birth to become the follower of Marwood, for, extraordinary though it may seem, the Chief Constable of Bradford was setting out to ask me to take the job at the very moment I was setting out to ask him to use his influence with the people of London.

A bizarre revelation indeed.

During Berry's reign as hangman a brass eyelet was spliced into the rope so that a more efficient, free running noose could be made.

Although there is no evidence for the assertion, Berry is reputed to have said that Bury was known to be Jack the Ripper. According to Berry, he was approached after the execution by two 'well suited gentleman', presumably from Scotland Yard, who told him,

> You'll find there will be no Whitechapel murders after this. You've put an end to Jack the Ripper's games.

Thomas 'Tam' Young   (Matthew Clydesdale)

Young, the man who executed Matthew Clydesdale, was employed by the City of Glasgow, although he did work elsewhere in Scotland when required.

His duties were to carry out prescribed sentences

> whether the same be capital or shall consist of whipping criminal, putting them in the pillory, or in the stocks, exposing them upon the platform.

In addition, he worked as a labourer at the jail and for his duties he was paid a salary of £50 per annum and had a free house, coals and candles, a free pair of shoes twice per year and a guinea (£1.05) for each execution he performed, all of which must have made him one of the best-paid executioners of the time.

He executed Hardie and Baird, whose only crimes were to be the men seen as the ringleaders of the radical reform movement, at Stirling in 1820, for which he was paid £50 plus expenses.

William Marwood

Marwood carried out a number of executions in Scotland, although there is no record of him performing any in Angus or Dundee.

He is worthy of mention however as the man who introduced scientific technique into the technology of hanging. It seems likely that Marwood got his ideas from others but, be that as it may, he was the man who revolutionised the whole unsavoury business.

Until then, wrongdoers had invariably been strangled rather than humanely executed. His breakthrough was to realise that a longer drop, with the knot placed at the main artery, would break the prisoner's neck and so result in almost instant death rather than the hideous slow procedure of the past.

This method, which brought a measure of science into the gruesome technology of hanging by taking factors such as the prisoner's height, weight, age and physical condition, into account in calculating the drop, was quickly adopted by the authorities.

Like Calcraft, Marwood was a shoemaker and he is said to have used a trapdoor at his warehouse to perfect his technique.

Marwood took his business seriously and he had total faith in the belief that hanging as a punishment prevented further murders and he was also the foremost executioner of his day, responsible for eliminating many of the most infamous criminals of the time.

A well known joke of the period was:

If pa killed ma, who would kill pa?

The answer was Marwood!

25 *Portrait of James Berry – the frontispiece to his book* My Experiences as an Executioner *(Bradford & London: Percy Lund & Co, 1892)*

Bibliography

Adams, Norman. *Hangman's Brae* (Edinburgh: Black & White Publishing Ltd, 2003)

Black, C Stewart. *Glasgow's Story* (Paisley: J & J Cook Ltd)

Cockburn, Lord Henry. *Circuit Journeys* (Edinburgh: David Douglas, 1889)

Emsley, John. *Elements of Murder: A History of Poison* (Oxford: OUP, 2005)

Gordon, Anne. *Death is for the Living* (Edinburgh: Paul Harris Publishing, 1984)

Grewar, David. *The Story of Glenisla* (Aberdeen: Milne & Hutchison, 1926)

Livingstone, Sheila. *Confess and Be Hanged* (Edinburgh: Birlinn, 2000)

Lowson, A. *Tales, Legends and Traditions of Forfarshire* (Forfar: John Macdonald, 1891)

Macpherson, Euan. *The Trial of Jack the Ripper* (Edinburgh: Mainstream Publishing, 2005)

Miller, A H. *Haunted Dundee* (Dundee: Malcolm C McLeod, 1923)

Roughead, William. *Twelve Scots Trials* (Edinburgh: The Mercat Press, 1995)

Sword, J. *They Did Wrong: Public Hangings in the Angus Area 1785 to 1868* (Dundee: Friends of Dundee City Archives)

Tod, T M. *The Scots Black Kalendar* (Perth: Munro & Scott, 1938)

Wade, Stephen. *Britain's Most Notorious Hangmen* (Barnsley: Pen & Sword Books, 2009)

Whittington-Egan, Molly. *Classic Scottish Murder Stories* (Glasgow: Neil Wilson Publishing, 2007)

Young, A F. *The Encyclopaedia of Scottish Executions 1750 to 1963* (Orpington: Eric Dobby Publishing, 1998)

Newspapers

The Dundee Advertiser

The Dundee Courier

The Montrose Review